Faith, Culture and the Dual System

Faith, Culture and the Dual System

A Comparative Study of Church and County Schools

Bernadette O'Keeffe
King's College, London

The Falmer Press
(A member of the Taylor & Francis Group)
London, New York and Philadelphia

UK	The Falmer Press, Falmer House, Barcombe, Lewes, East Sussex. BN8 5DL.
USA	The Falmer Press, Taylor & Francis Inc., 242 Cherry Street, Philadelphia. PA 19106-1906.

©1986 B. O'Keeffe

All rights reserved. No part of this publication may be reproduced, stored in a retrieval system, or transmitted in any form or by any means, electronic, mechanical, photocopying, recording or otherwise, without permission in writing from the Publisher.

First published in 1986

Library of Congress Cataloging-in-Publication Data

O'Keeffe, Bernadette.
 Faith, culture, and the dual system.

   1. Church schools — United States. 2. County school systems — United States. 3. Religious education — United States. 4. Intercultural education — United States. 5. Comparative education. I. Title.
LC427.034 1986   377   86-13391
ISBN 1-85000-110-3
ISBN 1-85000-111-1 (pbk.)

Typeset in 11/13 Caledonia by
Imago Publishing Ltd, Thame, Oxon

Printed in Great Britain by Taylor & Francis (Printers) Ltd, Basingstoke.

Contents

		Page
List of Tables		vi
Acknowledgements		ix
Introduction		x
Chapter 1	Setting the Scene	1
Chapter 2	Admissions Policies	17
Chapter 3	Admissions for Change	31
Chapter 4	Aspects of Diversity	55
Chapter 5	School Worship and Assemblies	69
Chapter 6	Religious Education	89
Chapter 7	Multicultural Education	127
Conclusion		151
Appendices		153
Interview Schedules and Questionnaires		165

List of Tables

		Pages
1	Details of the total sample of church and county schools in the study	7
2	Sample of teachers interviewed	8
3	Number of pupils in English state maintained schools — January 1983	11
4	Number of maintained schools in England — January 1983	12
5	Characteristics of voluntary aided and controlled schools	14
6	Religious affiliation of pupils in church secondary schools	23
7	Primary schools and parishes served by church secondary schools	25
8	Headteachers' replies in county and church secondary schools to the question: does the pupil intake reflect the neighbourhood composition?	26
9	Admissions criteria for church primary schools	27
10	Percentage distribution on religious backgrounds of pupils attending primary schools	28
11	Parents' reasons for selecting a Church of England secondary school	38
12	Percentage of teachers in church schools who are members of the Church of England	56
13	Percentage of pupils eligible for free school meals in a sample of country and church schools	60
14	Percentage of pupils eligible for free school meals in a sample of church secondary and primary schools	61
15	Percentage of pupils from single-parent families in a sample of church and county schools	61
16	Percentage of pupils from single-parent families in a sample of church secondary and primary schools	62

List of Tables

17	Cross-tabulation of parental occupations of pupils in a sample of county and church schools	63
18	Cross-tabulation of parental occupations of pupils in a sample of church secondary and primary schools	64
19	Quota of pupils in bands 1, 2, 3 in church and county schools	65
20	Cross-tabulation on the frequency of assembly for pupils in county and church schools	70
21	Frequency of assemblies for the whole school	71
22	Cross-tabulation of headteachers' classification of assemblies	71
23	Cross-tabulation of the Christian content in school assemblies	72
24	Cross-tabulation on aims of assembly in county and church schools	75
25	Frequencies for church-related activities in church secondary schools	82
26	Percentage distribution of religious education provision in county and church secondary schools	90
27	Cross-tabulation of the number of secondary schools and incidence of religious education lessons per week	91
28	Status of RE in the school curriculum	92
29	RE teachers' replies in secondary schools to the question: as a result of RE what do you hope to achieve for pupils by the time they leave school?	95
30	Replies to the question: do you think that an aim of RE is to nuture the personal faith of pupils?	98
31	RE teachers' view on the statement: RE that is concerned with Christian nurturing and teaching for commitment is justified within a community of faith because the child is better able to understand other religions	100
32	RE teachers' replies to the question: as a result of RE do you hope that pupils will have a clear understanding of Christian morality?	103
33	Specific provision for the study of world religions in secondary schools	104
34	Headteachers' replies concerning the aims and objectives of RE in primary schools	111
35	Parents' replies to the question: as a result of RE what do you hope this school will achieve for your child by the time he leaves school?	114
36	RE teachers' views of whether religious education should	117

List of Tables

      differ in church and county schools in aims, content and approach
37 Secondary headteachers' replies to the question: what in your view are the aims and purposes of multicultural education?   131
38 Details of progress in developing multicultural education in secondary schools   133
39 Primary headteachers' replies to the question: what progress has been made in your school in developing multicultural education?   143

Acknowledgements

My thanks are expressed to All Saints Educational Trust who funded the research project. In particular, I would like to express my appreciation to all of the Steering Committee members who took an active interest in every stage of the research, including the Research Directors, Professor David Aspin and Professor Stewart Sutherland. My warm thanks go to Dr. Sandra Williams for her contribution to the research. It was her enthusiasm and thoroughness which extended the scope of the research to include the North West Region and the West Midlands.

I would like to thank Peter Tedder for his help in preparing the data collected for computer analysis.

I wish to acknowledge the important contribution of the Directors of Education and their staff together with the Diocesan Directors of Education for granting research facilities and in providing the necessary information to enable us to select a sample of schools.

I am particularly indebted to headteachers and religious education teachers for sparing so much time to answer our questions. My thanks also go to all the teachers who were kind enough to complete and return their questionnaires.

My gratitude also extends to all parents who were willing to be interviewed.

Finally, I would like to thank Louise Wakefield, Dawn Jarvis and her staff for typing the manuscript.

Introduction

This study sets out to explore how church schools see their role in a multicultural, multiracial and multifaith society. Church schools are studied alongside county schools as partners in the 'dual system'.

The study falls into four main areas. First, it looks at schools and their pupil intake. It examines pupil admissions policies and the criteria used for admitting pupils. Different admissions policies are analyzed illustrating their effect both within the school context and on the neighbourhood as a whole. It looks at whether schools are responsive to the demands of the local community, or otherwise. In doing so, it tries to ascertain what admissions policies are implicitly or explicitly saying in terms of the criteria used for admitting pupils.

Second, it looks at the policies and practices adopted by church school governors in appointing teaching staff.

The third area deals with school worship, assembly and religious education and their place in the life of the school. It looks at some of the difficulties of implementing the law relating to the daily act of worship and why some schools observe the law while others disregard it. The research highlights the issues and challenges facing schools in a variety of school contexts — in situations where there are large numbers of pupils with different faiths; where the majority of children may come from Christian backgrounds but have tenuous church associations; and where the majority of pupils and their parents may be active members in the Church of England and the minority of pupils are of other faiths or of no faith. It looks at the current practices and what headteachers perceive as the appropriate form of school worship or assembly for their schools. Their answers illustrate not only pluralism arising from different faiths but the pluralism within Christianity itself.

A number of fundamental issues are presented which are seen to be relevant to the teaching of religious education. These include the place

Introduction

and justification of religious education in the curriculum and what religious education teachers see as an adequate religious education; what role religious education is seen as playing in multicultural education; and finally the role for religious education in multifaith schools and in predominatly Christian schools. It looks at teachers' arguments for and against the view that Christianity should be given a central place in religious education. The study also explains what religious education teachers hope to achieve for pupils by the time they leave school as a result of religious education.

The fourth main area which looks at multicultural education in schools sets out the views expressed by headteachers concerning the purposes of multicultural education and illustrates whether headteachers are convinced of the need to introduce it into the school curriculum. It looks at the educational response of the schools in the study to cultural diversity by considering at what changes have occurred in each school and in the curriculum in developing multicultural education. In doing so, it looks at whether headteachers see multicultural education as relevant to each school whatever the pupils' backgrounds or whether it is confined to those schools having pupils drawn from a variety of cultural backgrounds.

These four areas were identified as key areas for research in an attempt to discover how schools are responding to the presence of children from different cultures and faiths. The study makes no claim to these being the only areas where responses of schools can be measured. On the contrary other areas of research have a direct bearing but have not been included in the study, due to the limitations of time and resources.

While the study of church schools was the major impetus for establishing the research project, the importance of county schools' participation in the project cannot be over-stressed. They provide the context for comparison by delineating or establishing similarities and differences and allowing for an explanation of differences and similarities wherever they arise. A major advantage of this comparative approach is that it makes possible a dialectic between church and county schools.

In 1981 when our research project was established at King's College London, church schools were at the centre of a wide-ranging debate. Today, the situation has not changed. Their function is being debated by pressure groups, educationalists and politicians as well as within the churches themselves. Christians are divided about what church schools should symbolize and who they should provide for.

A major research objective was, therefore, a thorough grasp of facts in an attempt to widen the gap between 'seems' and 'is'. A systematic

Introduction

observation leading to insights into 'what is' can only be achieved by empirical enquiry.

In addition to ascertaining what is happening in the areas outlined earlier it has been an important research task to reach behind the policies, practices and behaviour and to grasp 'the level of meaning' by posing the 'why' question. Interviews with headteachers, religious education teachers and parents provide a context in which 'the level of meaning' can be explored.

Chapter 1

Setting the Scene

This study is based on research carried out in a sample of county secondary schools and a sample of Church of England primary and secondary schools with a voluntary-aided status. To facilitate an understanding of local requirements each Church of England voluntary-aided secondary school in the sample was paired with the closest Church of England primary school, and wherever possible the closest county school. The criterion of geographical proximity was essential in order to look at a cluster of schools serving approximately the same neighbourhood.

Throughout the research the focus was on secondary schools and not on the DES category of 'middle deemed secondary' schools.

In pairing schools the characteristics of secondary schools were matched as closely as possible, taking into account such factors as to the type of school, for example, whether it was grammar or comprehensive and the pupil composition — whether it had a single sex or mixed pupil intake.

Fieldwork in schools commenced in October 1982 and was completed in July 1984. The fieldwork was planned, and as far as possible, carried out in three separate stages: (i) the Inner London Education Authority; (ii) the outer London boroughs; and (iii) the North West Region and the West Midlands.

The Inner London Education Authority

In order to avoid any bias arising from the selection of schools all eighteen Church of England voluntary-aided secondary schools were invited to participate in the research and all agreed to cooperate.[1]

The matching church primary schools were identified with the help of the Deputy Schools Officer, Mr. J. Griffiths, of the London and Southwark Diocesan Boards of Education (this body has since been reorganized into two separate boards, one for London and one for Southwark). One of the primary schools was the closest match for two of the church secondary schools, thus reducing the number of church primary schools involved to seventeen. All of the church primary schools selected were also able to cooperate with us on the project.

Although the Inner London Education Authority approved the research, restrictions were placed on the choice of county secondary schools. Permission was not given to visit schools which had amalgamated in the last three years or were likely to amalgamate in the near future; a significant restriction in a situation of heavy falling rolls. The main reason given for this condition was that these schools would be experiencing a large volume of work due to reorganization.

Taking these restrictions into account, it was possible with the help of a Senior Research Officer in the Inner London Education Authority to match twelve of the eighteen church secondary schools with a county secondary school. In a few cases the county schools selected, although always in roughly the same area, were not always geographically the closest schools. Ten of these schools took part in the project, although one did so by postal communication rather than personal interview. The other two schools, while in sympathy with the general aims of the study, were unable to participate, either because of lack of time due to other commitments, or because of staffing difficulties.

Outer London Boroughs

From Department of Education and Science statistics ten outer London boroughs were identified as having one or more Church of England voluntary-aided secondary school in their authority.[2] These were: Barnet, Bromley, Croydon, Ealing, Enfield, Haringey, Havering, Hillingdon, Hounslow and Sutton. With the exception of Barnet, which had two such schools, the other London boroughs contained one each, giving a total of eleven schools. All of these church schools took part in the project.

With the help of the local education authorities and the appropriate Diocesan Education Officers the research plan requiring a matching of each church secondary school with the closest Church of England voluntary-aided primary school and, as far as possible, the closest county secondary school was followed. In all cases it was possible to identify a suitable primary school and all of these took part in the

Setting the Scene

project. Similarly, with the exception of Ealing, the cooperation of the closest county secondary school was also gained. The London Borough of Ealing Education Department was unable to match the only Church of England aided secondary school with a county school since the area was experiencing falling pupil rolls and was also subject to much secondary reorganization.

The North West Region and the West Midlands

Geographical Areas

At this stage of selecting the sample decisions had to be made concerning the choice of Church of England voluntary-aided secondary schools. Although a comprehensive survey of all Church of England voluntary-aided secondary schools had been feasible for the Inner London Education Authority and the outer London boroughs, limits on time and funding foreclosed this option for the rest of England. Furthermore, the intention of extending the project was not to survey all Church of England voluntary-aided schools but to look at variations from the London experience. This is not to infer a homogeneity of experience shared by church schools in London. Headteachers were keen to point out their differences in terms of location and pupil intake. Indeed, choices were made on two levels. First, the selection of geographical areas and secondly within these areas, which schools to visit.

It was ascertained from the DES statistics that there are seventeen Church of England voluntary-aided secondary schools in Metropolitan districts and forty of these schools in non-Metropolitan counties, giving a total of fifty-seven Church of England voluntary-aided secondary schools outside the Greater London area. This total does not include the DES category 'middle deemed secondary' schools. These fifty-seven schools are distributed between twelve Metropolitan districts and twenty non-Metroplitan counties. Metropolitan districts and non-Metropolitan counties are the tiers of local government responsible for the provision of education.[3]

As the project brief was primarily directed at an examination of church schools in a multifaith, multicultural and multiracial society priority was given to geographical areas which contained Church of England voluntary-aided secondary schools and which best approximated this description in terms of population composition. In order to identify these areas a table was constructed giving the distribution of Church of

Faith, Culture and the Dual System

England voluntary-aided secondary schools throughout England by government region and by local education authority, showing for each local education authority selected characteristics of the population which were critical for the project.[4]

Critical characteristics

The characteristics selected were derived from the 1981 census data,[5] the National Dwelling and Housing Survey,[6] and a DES Statistical Bulletin (8/82) concerned with 'A Classification of Local Education Authorities by Additional Educational Needs' (Cluster Analysis).

The indicators taken from the census data concern the country in which individuals were born and were twofold: firstly, the percentage of the usually resident population in households with the head of the household born in the New Commonwealth or Pakistan (NCWP); and secondly, the percentage of the usually resident population born outside the United Kingdom. The population of NCWP origin is defined (in terms used by the Office of Population, Censuses and Surveys) to include both persons wholly of NCWP origin and those of mixed origin, for example, children with one parent of NCWP origin and the other parent being a member of the indigenous population of Britain. Although this country of birth classification tends to under-state the total population of NCWP origin in areas where the NCWP population has been settled the longest and persons of NCWP ethnic origins who were born in the UK have established their own households, it is estimated by the Office of Population, Censuses and Surveys that:

> ... the indicator *persons in households with NCWP-born head*, given by the 1981 Census seems to provide a reasonable approximation to the size of the population of NCWP origin, including those of mixed origin, not only at the national level but also for Greater London as a whole, and by implication for other large concentrations of the NCWP population.[7]

To overcome some of the problems arising from the country of birth classification the government proposed to include a question on race or ethnic origin in the 1981 census (White Paper, Cmnd. 7146). However, tests using a variety of question designs and consultation with representatives of ethnic minority groups suggested that a question on race or ethnic origin would be unacceptable in a statutory census and would not produce accurate information. Consequently the government dropped this proposal.

Setting the Scene

It is of interest to record that during the test surveys carried out to develop a question of ethnic origin the Office of Population Censuses and Surveys found that, 'some Indians, Pakistanis and Bangladeshis felt that to define their ethnicity adequately one had to record both their place of origin **and** their religion'.[8] It follows, therefore, that the understanding of 'ethnic group' is not simply a group of people with distinctive physical characteristics such as skin colour, but rather a group of people sharing a particular culture in which religion is a major part.

Information from the census was supplemented with information about birthplace and ethnic origin given by the 1977–78 National Dwelling and Housing Survey. This source not only estimates the percentage of the population located in the various regions born outside of the UK, but also provides a useful breakdown in terms of ethnic group percentages in each region — comprising the categories of 'White, West Indian, African, Indian/Pakistani/Bangladeshi, and Other'.

Finally, information from the DES Statistical Bulletin 8/82 was used. This estimates socio-economic disadvantages and educational need in the local education authorities as reflected by six socio-economic indicators, selected both for their relevance to educational deprivation and the availability of reasonably recent data. The indicator most relevant to the project and the one which was recorded in addition to the overall cluster group code[9] was the percentage of children in each of the local education authorities 'born outside the UK or belonging to non-white ethnic groups'. In addition to children of West Indian, African, Indian, Pakistani or Bangladeshi origin, this category contains white English-speaking children born overseas. It would have been helpful to have had more direct and detailed information on the distribution of children from ethnic minority groups, but whilst individual authorities might collect statistics, which they may or may not be willing to reveal, this information has not been collected centrally since the DES collected statistics on immigrant pupils in 1972.[10]

Selection of areas

On the basis of available information presented in this table, and guided by information provided by a member of HMI of schools (with a specialism in multicultural education), two areas were selected for inclusion in the project. These are located in the North West region and the West Midlands. They comprise the following local education authorities:

Faith, Culture and the Dual System

1. *North West Region:* the metropolitan districts of Bolton and Oldham, and three non-Metropolitan districts in Lancashire local education authority — Blackburn, Preston and neighbouring South Ribble;
2. *West Midlands:* the Metropolitan districts of Birmingham and Wolverhampton.

Within these two areas the focus is primarily on local education authorities with relatively high concentrations of ethnic minority groups and which also contain Church of England voluntary-aided secondary schools. Some other local education authorities may have higher concentrations of ethnic minorities, but are not included because they do not have Church of England voluntary-aided secondary schools.

Schools

The seven Metropolitan or non-Metropolitan districts listed under the two regions included a total of nine Church of England voluntary-aided secondary schools; Bolton (1), Oldham (2), Blackburn (1), Preston (1), South Ribble (1), Birmingham (2), Wolverhampton (1). To avoid a bias in selection of schools, all were invited to take part in the project. Following the pattern used in London, each of these schools was matched with the closest Church of England voluntary-aided primary school and, as far as possible, the closest county secondary school, giving a maximum of twenty-seven schools for research outside of London. Without exception, all participated in the survey.

Controlling local education and diocesan authorities

Inclusion of a school in the sample was dependent on the approval of the relevant local education authority and the Headteacher and, in the case of Church schools, approval by the Diocesan Director of Education and the School Governors. The following local education authorities and dioceses were involved in the research:

Local Education Authorities — Inner London Education Authority, Barnet, Bromley, Croydon, Ealing, Enfield, Haringey, Havering, Hillingdon, Hounslow, Sutton, Bolton, Oldham, Lancashire (covering Blackburn, Preston, South Ribble), Birmingham and Wolverhampton.
Dioceses — London, Southwark, Canterbury (detached), Chelmsford, Rochester, Blackburn, Manchester, Birmingham, Lichfield.

Setting the Scene

Total sample

The total sample consisted of 103 schools, involving sixteen local education authorities and nine dioceses. The schools were distributed as follows:

TABLE 1: *Details of the total sample of Church and County Schools in the study*

	Inner London Education Authority	Outer London boroughs	Rest of England	All areas
Church of England aided secondary	18[1]	11	9	38
Church of England aided primary	17[2]	11	9	37
County secondary	9[3]	10[4]	9	28
All schools	45	32	27	103

Notes
1 This total includes a church school which was voluntary-aided at the time of interview, but has since become voluntary-controlled.
2 One of the primary schools was the closest match for two of the church secondary schools, thus reducing the number of church primary schools in the Inner London Education Authority involved to seventeen instead of eighteen.
3 Taking into account the Inner London Education Authority's restrictions placed on us, it was possible to match twelve of the eighteen church secondary schools with a county secondary school. Ten of these agreed to take part in the project, but interviews at one school did not materialise. Interview schedules were left for completion by the headteacher and the religious education teacher at the school but these were not returned. Duplicate sets of schedules were sent but they were returned partially completed. At this point it was decided not to include the school in the sample.
4 Research was carried out in ten instead of the planned eleven county secondary schools in the outer London boroughs because the London Borough of Ealing was unable to match its one Church of England voluntar aided secondary school with a county secondary school.

Sample of teachers

One hundred and two headteachers in secondary and primary schools were interviewed. In addition, interviews were carried out among sixty-seven religious education teachers (or their equivalent — for example, Head of Social Studies, where religious education is integrated into a social studies programme). The following table gives further details.

In addition to these planned interviews informal discussions occurred frequently with a range of staff including deputy heads, heads of departments and subject teachers.

Most visits to schools by the project team included a tour of the schools. These proved to be a very important part of the research since such occasions provided an opportunity to get the general atmosphere of the school to observe the kinds of things that were rewarded, celebrated and emphasized. Invitations by headteachers to observe school worship

TABLE 2: Sample of teachers interviewed

School type	Headteachers	Religious education teachers
Church of England aided secondary	38[1]	39[2]
Church of England aided primary	36[3]	n/a[4]
County secondary	28[5]	28
All schools	102	67

Notes
1 This total includes one acting head.
2 In one school *both* the Head of Religious Education and the Head of Divinity were interviewed increasing the expected total of religious education teachers in Church of England voluntary-aided secondary schools from thirty-eight to thirty-nine.
3 This total excludes one church primary school where the questions were completed by post.
4 Not applicable because no religious education teachers were interviewed in primary schools.
5 This total includes three acting heads and also one long-standing deputy head who was interviewed in preference to a newly-appointed headmaster who was unfamiliar with the school.

and to attend church services were accepted. All observations were recorded by the project team.

In each of the secondary schools visited self-completion postal questionnaires were given to the headteacher to distribute to a 10 per cent sample of teachers. The headteacher was asked to select every tenth name on the register of teachers. If, however, this method resulted in too many teachers in the same age group or from similar backgrounds the headteacher was asked to select the name of the teacher immediately before or after the tenth name.

A total of 139 parents who had a child/children at a Church of England voluntary-aided secondary school were interviewed. These interviews were carried out in seven of the church schools involved in the project in the Greater London area. In two schools interviews took place with parents of first year pupils and in the remaining with parents of prospective pupils. All parents invited to participate in the project agreed to do so.

Invitations to attend three governors' meetings in church schools were accepted. In addition meetings took place with a number of school governors. These included five chairmen of governing bodies, two vice-chairmen and several long-standing members.

Response rate

The response rate for headteachers and religious education teachers in church schools was 100 per cent. In county schools, while yielding a lower response rate than church schools, the level of response was still

Setting the Scene

remarkably high at 90 per cent. The response rate for the overall sample was 97 per cent.

The response rate for completion of postal questionnaires was again very high. Three hundred and eighty-one questionnaires were given to headteachers to distribute and 317 were received giving a response rate of 83 per cent.

Four interview schedules and two questionnaires were designed for collecting information relating to the main areas outlined earlier. The majority of questions in the interview schedule used during interviews with headteachers in county and church secondary schools were identical. In addition, a number of questions were included which had specific relevance for either type of school.

While many of the questions in the interview schedule used for headteachers in primary schools were the same as those for secondary schools, there were additional questions concerning the teaching of religious education.

A single interview schedule was used for collecting information from religious education teachers in both church and county schools.

An appropriately designed interview schedule was also used when talking to parents about their reasons for choosing a church school for their son or daughter.

The questions in all schedules were, in the main, open-ended. This type of question provided a greater opportunity for exploring an individual's experience and it enabled the participant to express this in his/her own words.

The staff postal questionnaire was designed to find out what are the perceptions and expectations of teachers concerning church schools. It consisted of forty statements made about church schools and teachers were asked to indicate whether they agreed or disagreed with the statements. Some questions related to the desirability of the Church of England's involvement in education and other questions related to the contribution of church schools to education; yet others dealt with church schools and their accountability, autonomy and decision-making; while others were concerned with the implications of church schools' policies, such as admissions policy.[11]

Additional information was collected concerning the age, sex, religious affiliation and teaching experience of teachers completing the questionnaires.

A questionnaire was sent to each of the local education authorities who had participated in the research. The questionnaire was designed to collect information in three areas. First, details on pupil admission policies for county schools. Secondly, information was requested on what provision had been made for multicultural education. Details of multicultural education policies and resource centres were requested. In addition they were asked whether Section II teachers, ESL teachers or teachers to develop communication skills in the mother tongue were employed, and where they were, the number of teachers involved.

Information was also sought as to whether statistics were collected by the local education authorities on the ethnic composition of the total pupil population and if this was the case whether the authorities would be prepared to provide details of these statistics together with the ethnic composition of individual schools in the project.

Diocesan Directors of Education were sent a questionnaire for completion. The areas covered included admissions policies, the role of the church schools, church schools and accountability, diocesan initiatives and the number of church schools in each diocese.

Preliminary Survey

Before undertaking fieldwork it was necessary to ascertain the adequacy of the information gathering techniques to be employed by testing interview schedules and self-completion postal questionnaires. This preliminary work also provided the opportunity to gauge the response of teachers and to estimate the time required to complete interview schedules.

A Church of England primary and secondary school were visited for this purpose. The headteachers were interviewed and in the case of the secondary school the Head of the Religious Education Department. A self-completion postal questionnaire was distributed to a 10 per cent sample of teachers in that secondary school.

Headteachers showed a general spirit of helpfulness and enthusiasm for our research which was illustrated by their willingness to allocate a complete afternoon to talk and answer questions. The response from teachers at this preliminary stage in completing the postal questionnaires was 100 per cent.

As a result of the preliminary survey the interview schedule and postal questionnaires were revised.

In each selected area where there were Church of England voluntary-aided secondary schools the method was to carry out research in all these schools. This resulted in a total sample of all such schools in the local education authority and avoided any bias arising from selection. This, however, was not the case for church primary schools and county schools. In the case of primary schools and county secondary

Setting the Scene

schools they were selected on the basis of geographical proximity to the church secondary school and not on how representative they were of county and church primary school provision within the particular local education authority. It is not possible, therefore, to talk about these schools as being representative of schools in the local education authority. The sample design enables us to look at the activities of the schools within a geographical area.

While the sample of Church of England voluntary aided secondary schools represented 42.6 per cent of all Church of England secondary schools with a voluntary-aided status (excluding schools 'middle deemed secondary') at the time the research was undertaken the county school sample represented less than 1 per cent of county school provision. The Church of England primary school sample represented 1.9 per cent of all Church of England voluntary-aided primary schools (excluding 'deemed primary').

Tables 3 and 4 provide statistics on the number of maintained schools in England and the pupil population.

Church of England schools provide for 17.5 per cent of primary school pupils with 7.6 per cent of these pupils being educated in a voluntary-aided primary school. At secondary level, 4.1 per cent of all

TABLE 3: *Number of pupils in English state-maintained schools — January 1983*

		PRIMARY Number	Percentage of total primary pupil nos.	SECONDARY Number	Percentage of total secondary pupil nos.	TOTAL Number	Percentage of total pupil nos.
All Schools		3,749,694	100	3,740,944	100	7,490,638	100
County	Total	2,718,515	72.5	3,107,100	83.0	5,825,615	77.77
Voluntary	Total	1,031,179	27.5	633,844	17.0	1,665,023	22.23
	Controlled	382,167	10.2	166,925	6.5	549,092	7.03
	Aided	649,013	17.3	466,919	12.5	1,115,932	14.89
C.E.	Total	657,711	17.5	156,919	4.1	814,630	10.87
	Controlled	370,553	9.9	63,990	1.7	434,543	5.80
	Aided	287,158	7.6	92,929	2.4	380,087	5.07
Roman Catholic		352,929	9.4	336,003	8.9	688,932	9.19
Methodist	Total	5,048	0.13	–	–	5,084	0.06
	Controlled	4,384	0.11	–	–	4,384	0.05
	Aided	664	0.01	–	–	664	–
Jewish	Aided	4,440	0.01	3,187	0.08	7,627	0.10
Other Voluntary	Total	11,052	0.29	137,735	3.6	148,787	1.98
	Controlled	7,187	0.19	102,935	2.7	110,122	1.47
	Aided	3,865	0.10	34,800	0.9	38,665	0.51

Notes:
1 All figures are taken from DES Statistical Table A913 [A10/82].
2 'Aided' category includes 'Special Agreement' schools.
3 The one RC controlled primary school has been included in the aided category: it has thirty-nine pupils.
4 Middle schools have been merged into either the primary or secondary category on the basis of the DES designation of each school
5 Figures for primary schools are full-time equivalent. Part-time pupils (all under 5) are counted as 0.5 of a full-time pupil.

11

TABLE 4: Number of maintained schools in England — January 1983

	Primary	Deemed primary	Percentage of total primary	Secondary	Deemed secondary	Percentage of total secondary schools	Total number	Percentage of total schools
All Schools	19,604	757	100	3,905	648	100	24,914	100
County Total	12,634	626	65.1	3,121	522	80.0	16,903	67.8
Voluntary Total	6,970	131	34.8	784	126	19.9	8,011	32.01
Voluntary Controlled	3,025	61	15.1	172	47	4.8	3,305	13.02
Voluntary Aided	3,943	70	19.7	525	68	13.0	4,606	18.04
Special Agreement	2	—	0.0	87	11	2.1	100	0.40
Church of England								
Total	4,925	102	24.6	159	82	5.2	5,268	21.01
Controlled	2,938	61	14.7	56	46	2.2	3,101	12.04
Aided	1,986	41	9.9	89	31	2.6	2,147	8.06
Special Agreement	1	—	0.0	14	5	0.4	20	0.08
Roman Catholic								
Total	1,919	28	9.5	452	42	10.8	2,441	9.07
Controlled	1	—	0.0	—	—	—	1	0.00
Aided	1,917	28	9.5	380	36	9.1	2,361	9.04
Special Agreement	1	—	0.0	72	6	1.7	79	0.31
Methodist								
Total	38	—	0.18	—	—	—	38	0.15
Controlled	34	—	0.16	—	—	—	34	0.13
Aided	4	—	0.02	—	—	—	4	0.01
Special Agreement	—	—	—	—	—	—	—	—

Setting the Scene

Jewish							
Total	16	–	0.07	4	1	0.1	21	0.08
Controlled	–	–	–	–	–	–	–	–
Aided	16	–	0.07	3	1	0.1	20	0.08
Special Agreement	–	–	–	1	–	–	1	–
Other Voluntary								
Total	72	1	0.35	169	1	3.7	243	0.97
Controlled	52	–	0.25	116	1	2.5	169	0.67
Aided	20	1	0.10	53	–	1.2	74	0.29
Special Agreement	–	–	–	–	–	–	–	–

Notes:
1 All figures are taken from DES Statistical Table A9/83.
2 The statistics do not include ecumenical schools. There are twenty-three Anglican/Methodist primary schools and one primary and four secondary Anglican/Roman Catholic schools.

13

Faith, Culture and the Dual System

pupils are in a Church of England secondary school with 2.4 per cent of these pupils in aided secondary schools.

Roman Catholic schools provide for 9.4 per cent of the primary school population and for 9.0 per cent at secondary level.

Combining the statistics for primary and secondary schools the statistics show that five pupils in every 100 are in Church of England voluntary-aided schools and nine pupils in every 100 are in Roman Catholic voluntary-aided schools.

The differences between voluntary-aided and voluntary-controlled schools can be seen in table 5.

TABLE 5: *Characteristics of voluntary aided and controlled schools*

	Voluntary Aided	Voluntary Controlled
Composition of Governing Body	The majority are Foundation governors. If the governing body has eighteen members or less Foundation governors out-number other members by two and by three if it has more members.	One-fifth are Foundation governors. The majority are local authority governors.
School Buildings	Governors exercise full control.	LEA control.
Use of school premises outside school hours	Governors control.	LEA control.
Capital costs	15 per cent provided by governors.	Nil.
Staff appointments	Governors responsibility.	LEA responsibility (governors consulted over 'reserved teacher' for church teaching).
Pupil admissions	Governors responsibility.	LEA responsibility.
Religious education	Governors control in secondary schools. The governors have general oversight in primary schools	LEA agreed syllabus. Optional C of E teaching.
Curriculum	Responsibility of governors in secondary schools LEA in primary schools.	LEA.

Special agreement schools share the same characteristics of voluntary-aided schools. In addition, each will have a special agreement with the local education authority generally relating to the particular interest of school.

Table 5 illustrates that the differences between schools with a voluntary-aided and voluntary-controlled status relate to where the power and responsibilities rest. For aided schools the power and responsibilities are with the school governors whereas in controlled schools they rest with the local education authority.

With the exception of the teaching of religious education and the

Setting the Scene

provision of Church of England optional teaching for children whose parents request it; the provision for 'reserved' teachers and the composition of governing bodies voluntary controlled schools share the same characteristics of county schools.

These features of the dual system allow for diversity of responses among churches and state as partners in education.

Notes

1. One school is included in this total, but its current status as a Church of England voluntary-aided secondary school is uncertain. The London Diocese no longer include it in their list of schools and it could conceivably be classified as a Christian school and not a Church of England school.
2. DES computer print-out of table 1D/00 1981. This table actually records eight outer London boroughs as containing Church of England voluntary-aided secondary schools. It omits in error the London Borough of Hounslow, and does not include Ealing, which has only recently acquired a Church of England voluntary-aided secondary school.
3. In the course of identifying Church of England voluntary-aided secondary schools in the rest of England, we found three further errors in table 1D/00 1981. Shropshire should be recorded as having no Church of England voluntary-aided secondary schools, Kent has two such schools not three, and Oxfordshire has one such school, not two.
4. See table 3 in Appendix 1, 'Distribution of Church of England Voluntary-Aided Secondary Schools Outside Greater London — By Region/Local Education Authority, with selected characteristics of the population'. Similar information is provided for London schools in Appendix 1 (Tables 1 and 2).
5. *Census 1981:* selected data summarized in the Office of Population Censuses and Surveys County Monitors, a series of fifty-seven pamphlets published by the government statistical service.
6. *National Dwelling and Housing Survey:* Phase 1 (HMSO 1979), Phases 11 and 111 (HMSO 1980).
7. OPCS, (1982) Editorial, *Population Trends* 28, p. 6.
8. OPCS Monitor, Cen 78/4, 25 July 1978, p. 7.
9. Using the technique known as cluster analysis and adopting a particular similarity coefficient (alternative approaches and other similarity coefficients could have been used) this bulletin groups local education authorities into six relatively homogeneous groups, each with a cluster group code, A–F.
10. DES *(1972) Statistics of Education, Vol. 1, Schools,* Immigrant Pupils (table 34–38).
11. The results and analysis of this questionnaire are not dealt with in this book.

Chapter 2

Admissions Policies

This chapter looks at the arrangements for the admission of pupils to county and church schools. No attempt will be made in this chapter to give any detailed assessment of the effects of these policies. It gives us a springboard from which to initiate discussion of the main areas that have been the subject of the research.

As a result of the 1980 Education Act[1] parents are entitled to state a preference for any school which is controlled by their local education authority. With some authorities parents can express a preference for schools outside their jurisdiction.

Local education authorities and governors of church-aided schools must comply with that preference unless to do so would 'prejudice the provision of efficient education or the efficient use of resources'. There are exceptions, however, where a stated preference might be incompatible with existing agreements between the local education authority and governors of a voluntary-aided school, or in the case of a selective school where the child has not met the requirements based on academic ability and aptitude.

Parents of all pupils scheduled for transfer to a secondary school were provided with information about available schools within an area and they were given the opportunity to visit them. Parents were then asked to express their preferences (usually three) and to state reasons for their preferences.

The majority of local education authorities operate a catchment area policy which is defined in geographical terms resulting in an easily identifiable area. Normally, the home address determines the catchment area for a particular pupil.

Nine local education authorities, while endeavouring to place as many children as possible in schools which parents had selected give

Faith, Culture and the Dual System

first priority to children living in the neighbourhood of the school. When the needs of the neighbourhood are met and vacant places remain they are filled with children from other areas. Six authorities' admissions policies are committed to parental choice of secondary schools as a starting point. The remaining authority gives priority if there are siblings already attending the school. If county schools are oversubscribed, admissions are made using different priorities. No test was made of the effect of a neighbourhood school policy or its influence on the tone or academic success of schools. It is noteworthy that seventeen (61 per cent) of the twenty-eight county schools in the study were oversubscribed. There is considerable variation between authorities with some giving first priority to children who name a school as their first preference; others give first priority to children whose parents name the school for medical reasons; or where the child is attending the associated primary school or to siblings already attending the school.

All pupil admissions to county schools are handled centrally by the local education authority. With a few exceptions, the arrangements for pupil admissions are the same for all county schools in a given LEA. When pupils have been allocated places at county schools parents are notified and headteachers are sent a list of the names of pupils who have been allocated a place at their school. If parents are refused their preferred school they have the right to appeal against the decision.[2] In the case of admissions to selective schools in the study pupils are required to take an entrance examination and attend the school for an interview.

Only one headteacher in an all-ability county school interviews pupils before allocating places. He was concerned to find out more about the children because, he said 'primary school profiles were hopeless' if used as the sole basis for selection.

Before looking at admissions policies for church schools I want to outline the Church of England structure in church school provision.

There are three levels of Church of England involvement in education — first, on a national level; secondly on an area level; and thirdly, on a local level.

At the national level the National Society has a constitutional link with many church schools. Although it does exercise considerable influence its role is an advisory one. It provides legal advice to dioceses, or, where requested, to governing bodies of church schools. Guidance is given covering pupil admissions policies, finance, advice on religious education and general policy. While the National Society offers advice and makes recommendations it does not have any legal powers to implement policy.

Admissions Policies

There are close links between the National Society and the General Synod Board of Education. The DES looks to the National Society and the General Synod Board of Education for the Church of England view. In 1958 the Board of Education was established to promote and co-ordinate the work of the Church of England in the field of education. One of its main functions was to speak to the Church Assembly on general education policy. The Board of Education is the official voice of the Church of England on educational matters. Through its membership of the central Joint Education Policy Committee it is consulted by the DES on matters affecting church schools. While the Board of Education can exercise considerable influence its role, like that of the National Society, is an advisory role.

On an area level, each of the forty-three dioceses in England has a Diocesan Education Committee (DEC) which is responsible for looking after the interests of church schools within a geographically defined area — the Diocese. Generally speaking, the Bishop of the Diocese is Chairman of that Committee. The DEC enters into consultations and negotiations with the local education authority and the DES concerning school closures, reorganization or any changes directed at church school provision within its area. Legally it has no control over individual church schools but it can exercise a considerable amount of influence especially where it is involved in the building of a school or in the financial affairs of individual schools. Nevertheless, it has an advisory role only. It gives advice to trustees, owners, managers and governors of church schools where necessary. The governors of church schools must consult with the DEC concerning any major changes of policy, such as amalgamations, schools closures or change of school status. All Diocesan Education Committees had appointed representatives to the governing bodies of schools in the study. Each diocese through its Diocesan Education Committee has established a clear policy on admissions for church schools in the diocese. A clear policy statement on admissions in no way means its implementation in all Church schools. There is no obligation for individual schools to adopt the policy. Some governors continue to exercise 'the legal rights' of individual governing bodies in formulating their own criteria for admissions as the following comments from diocesan directors shows:

> In all but a very tiny minority of our schools this policy, which is agreed with the LEA of course, is not only followed but welcomed by governors. The tiny minority tend to emphasize the church links rather than those of the community and this occasionally causes problems.

> We try to administer the National Society's guidelines. The odd school doesn't and they exercise a very selective C of E policy and cause continual controversy.

Governing bodies of very popular over-subscribed schools, and schools that were not funded by a diocese but by endowments were the **most** likely to frustrate any move by the DEC to introduce an admissions policy for all its schools.

In addition to the limited powers of the DEC, what complicates the situation still further is the relationship that exists between the Diocesan Director, headteacher and governing body. Some Diocesan Directors see their role as 'visitors', other as 'an authority but not in authority' and still others as paymasters or administrators. One headteacher talked about the tensions that can occur when there is a lack of partnership and shared responsibility between the diocese and headteacher:

> Why should the diocese impose changes on us when they don't know what we are doing. We are one of their better schools ...
> The deputy headteacher said he (the Diocesan Director) wouldn't recognize me if he fell over me.

In church voluntary-aided schools the governors are responsible for formulating pupil admissions policies. The governing body of each school specifies its own admissions policy and decides its own criteria for admission. It is noteworthy that the independence afforded to church schools in determining admissions stems from their Articles of Government and the provisions laid down in the 1944 Education Act. Normally, this independence enables schools to fulfil the specific requirements of their Trust Deeds. Accordingly, the Articles of Government are not the same for all schools. As the National Society points out 'The Trust Deed on which a particular school was founded may stipulate an area of benefit — a parish or other area of residence for the benefit of those people the school came into being. It may also refer to the kind of religious practices and teaching the school was intended to uphold.'[3] In addition, governors must adhere to any agreement made with the local education authority concerning the distribution of pupils according to their range of ability. Parents wishing to send their child to a church voluntary-aided school were, in the majority of cases, instructed to make their application directly to the school they wished their child to attend.

During the enquiries associated with this project, headteachers were asked to provide us with details of their admissions policies. For Church secondary schools in the study, admissions policies are weighted in favour of a single criterion — that of religious affiliation. Thirty-three schools (87 per cent) give first priority to children from practising Anglican homes. Second priority is given to children whose parents are practising members of other Christian traditions.

One school gives first priority to parents wanting their child to be educated in a school that has a religious foundation — indeed whether these people were practising Christians is considered to be irrelevant. The emphasis on parents wanting an education for children which has a religious base enables this headteacher to reflect the diversity of the neighbourhood in the pupil intake. The pupil population represented 'nineteen nationalities, thirty countries or origin, twenty-two first languages, six Christian denominations, five other faiths, agnostics and atheists'. This school was over-subscribed by 32 per cent. Its school doors are 'open to all members of the community'. The admissions policy is based on the underlying philosophy that 'it is a real partner with the county schools and like the Church of England itself, accepts a "pastoral responsibility for all people of the land".'[4] Another two headteachers put the stress on Christian rather than Church of England affiliation. This criterion is not without its difficulties as one headteacher explained, 'There are problems here, if you have a regular Pentecostal and an infrequent Church of England attender which do you take? It is very difficult to decide'.

In addition, twenty-two headteachers (58 per cent) require an application for a place to be supported by a letter from a vicar stating that the parents and/or the child are active church members. The importance of the letter is illustrated by a headteacher in the following way. 'It is really on the strength of the vicar's recommendation of being active members of the Church of England that the child is accepted for the school. Both the child's and the parent's church involvement count but there is more of an emphasis on the child. The vicar is asked to rate the child's attendance in terms of a scale indicating good, average or casual attendance, A, B or C'.

Two schools put siblings first in the order of priority in the admissions criteria. However, as one headteacher pointed out, 'effectively this is a church membership criterion because most of the initial children entering the school would have been admitted under Church-related criteria'.

Most schools list criteria covering social and medical reasons, requests for church school education and special needs. In over-subscribed schools proximity to the school has very little relevance if unrelated to Church-related criteria. Schools vary in giving a higher priority to any of the categories. In addition, a number of schools have an 'others' category but this tends to be at the bottom of the list of criteria.

Only two headteachers explicitly mentioned criteria for children of other faiths. The application form for admissions to one of these schools had a section to be completed by 'a religious teacher for children of faiths other than Christianity'.

The extent of church connection is assessed in a variety of ways. Some schools take into consideration whether the prospective pupil is baptized or confirmed, whether the child is a weekly church attender. Schools operate a points system where points are allocated according to the amount of involvement in church activities by the parents and the child. They cover whether the child and parents regularly and frequently worship in a church; years of attendance at the church; child's and parents' involvement in other church activities. Separate scores are given for the child and the parents. In addition, points are given to a child attending a church primary school, or if the child is living near the school, whether there are siblings attending the school, other parental links with the school and medical and social reasons. When the points score has been ascertained for each child the governors then allocate places to those children reaching the appropriate qualifying score. This score can vary from year to year depending on how many applications are received.

It is in over-subscribed situations that the admissions criteria are applied rigidly. At the time the research was undertaken, thirty-one (82 per cent) out of the thirty-eight church secondary schools were over-subscribed. What happens in practice, is that when the school is over-subscribed, headteachers work down the list of criteria and in many instances they stop at the second. It is important however not to equate over-subscribed schools with applications from Anglicans only. There are only two secondary schools in the study which fill all their places with children from practising Anglican families. Table 6 shows the proportion of pupils with formal church connections and the proportion of children belonging to other faiths.

While in theory, the majority of church secondary schools gave first preference to practising members of the Anglican church, in practice, however, over half the schools in the study admitted pupils who were from other Christian traditions, other faiths and some pupils with no faith at all (table 6). Table 6 does not, however, give statistics for pupils with no religious affiliation. Except in two schools they were a relatively small minority.

Table 6 illustrates that seventeen schools (45 per cent) fill all their places with pupils who meet church-related criteria. What is significant

Admissions Policies

TABLE 6: *Religious affiliation of pupil in church secondary schools*

	Number of schools	Percentage
Anglicans only	2	5.2
All Christian — majority C of E	5	13.2
All Christian	10	26.4
Majority Christian	1	2.6
Majority Christian — one or two pupils of other faiths	11	29.1
Majority Christian — under 9 per cent other faiths	1	2.6
Majority Christian — 10–19 per cent other faiths	4	10.5
Majority Christian — 30–39 per cent other faiths	1	2.6
Majority Christian — 40–49 per cent other faiths	1	2.6
Majority other faiths and no faith	1	2.6
Majority no faith	1	2.6
Total	38	100.0

about this set of statistics is that it represents 19 per cent of all Church of England secondary schools with a voluntary-aided status (excluding 'middle deemed' secondary schools).[5]

For schools that are under-subscribed headteachers worked down the list of criteria to fill the spare places. These schools, by law, are required to take all children who apply for a place that is available. However, one headteacher whose school was under-subscribed refused to take a pupil who did not meet the church affiliation criteria.

Admissions policies for all schools in the Inner London Education Authority are further complicated by the fact that headteachers have to accept pupils in accordance with a 'balance of ability' formula given to them each year by the ILEA. Each school is required to take an agreed number of pupils in Band 1, Band 2 and Band 3. The three bands relate to the ability of the children — Band 1 refers to pupils graded as above average, Band 2 covers pupils of average ability and Band 3 are those pupils who are graded as below average.

While there is a good deal of variation, schools are generally required to take 25 per cent of pupils above average ability, 50 per cent of average ability and 25 per cent of pupils who were below average ability. Over-subscription had to be sorted out within each ability band.

Headteachers in over-subscribed schools were asked what changes would be made to admissions policies in the event that their schools became under-subscribed. Fourteen headteachers whose schools had always been over-subscribed said it was too hypothetical to even contemplate. Schools which fill up on church affiliation criterion said they would work further down their list of admissions criteria. Other headteachers said they would alter the admissions criteria if that was the only way the school could survive. One headteacher pointed out the dilemma facing headteachers.

> If we were under-subscribed I would be prepared to change the admissions criteria. If you are under-subscribed and do not alter the criteria you are accepting that your school will be reduced in size. However, you cannot win. At the moment we are accused by those who do not like church schools of not taking pupils who are not Christians. If we were under-subscribed and did not want to have unfilled places and then allowed more and more non-Christians in at a time of falling rolls when county schools are losing children, we could be accused of poaching children from them.

In nineteen (50 per cent) schools headteachers retain the right to interview pupils and, in some cases, parents as well. While the majority place an emphasis on the benefits of interviewing for the school the minority mentioned the benefits for the child.

The interview is seen as providing the opportunity to 'make sure the information on the application form is true'; 'it is the fairest way to apply our criteria; to get confirmation that the child will participate in the full life of the school' and 'to obtain additional information about the child'. One headteacher gave a slip of paper to parents asking them to list their reasons for applying. He pointed out that 'you could call this a test of intelligence for the parents. They may put down uniform or discipline etc., instead of a church school'.

Two headteachers who had discontinued interviewing decided to return to the practice because they found that 'the profiles on the children contained only verbal reasoning; there is nothing about family circumstances, social reasons, personality of the child and so on. This is not so that we can exclude non-Christians. We accept many children on social grounds whom we would not admit just on their profiles'. One headteacher talked about a Muslim mother who was separated from her husband but was too embarrassed to write this information in her application form. The view was also expressed that 'the articulate on paper are more likely to get the places'.

Headteachers who had discontinued the practice of interviewing were adamant in their condemnation and they highlighted some of 'the dangers'. The following abstracts illustrate the difficulties and dangers surrounding subjectivity when interviewing; 'I don't interview because I think if I had a child in front of me I would respond favourably to a bright, outgoing child and I think this is wrong. The results of interviewing might give a preponderance of bright, lively children. This is a weakness inherent in the system'. Another said 'I gave up interviewing because it was not the right way of selecting. Admissions can be carried out on paper. Once you see a child you are selecting on other than published admissions policy'. In general, headteachers who did not interview children relied heavily on the letter of recommendation from the vicar or minister.

Headteachers provided us with the opportunity to talk to parents when they attended the school for an interview. We found that for many pupils and parents, interviews did little to remove the anxiety which pupils felt about changing to a secondary school. It seemed that parents often shared their children's hopes and fears. Interviews were daunting for some children — some remained silent. For parents and children there was the fear of rejection or failure. Parents frequently said — 'I hope he hasn't failed'.

In the majority of local education authorities in the study most church secondary schools are drawing pupils from much wider areas than their matching county schools. First preference to Anglican children and second priority to Christian children result in situations where church secondary schools are drawing pupils from large numbers of primary schools. Not all headteachers were able to provide precise details of the areas served by their schools; they referred to the area as 'vast', 'colossal' or very wide catchment area. Others provided statistics on feeder primary schools or the number of parishes served by the school (See Table 7 below).

TABLE 7: Primary schools and parishes served by church secondary schools

Number of feeder Primary schools	Number of secondary schools
14	1
19	1
24	1
30–32	5
37	1
40–45	5
48	1
50–53	2
56–58	3
68–69	2
84	1
Number of parishes	
2	2
5	1
25	1
30	1
47	1
Very wide catchment area (no accurate statistics)	9
Total	38

Faith, Culture and the Dual System

TABLE 8: *Headteachers' replies in county and church secondary schools to the question — does the pupil intake reflect the neighbourhood composition?*

Replies	County Schools Number Percentage	Church Schools Numbers Percentage
Yes despite wide catchment area	15 (54)	8 (21)
Yes	6 (21)	2 (4)
Does not reflect neighbourhood composition	4 (14)	28 (75)
No — voluntary schools skew intake	1 (4)	— —
No grammar schools skew intake	2 (7)	— —
Total	28 (100)	38 (100)

It is not surprising, therefore, that only a minority of headteachers in church secondary schools said that their pupil intake reflects the neighbourhood composition. Table 8 gives the replies of headteachers in county and church secondary schools to the question — does the pupil intake reflect the neighbourhood composition?

The above table highlights not only the differences between county and church schools, but also the magnitude of the differences in reflecting the local community. While 75 per cent of county headteachers said that their pupil intake mirrors the nighbourhood, 75 per cent of headteachers in church schools said their pupil intake did not.

The point made by one county head that the local church voluntary school skews the county school intake will be developed in the following chapter.

When the statistics on over-subscribed church schools are compared with their matching county schools the results show that in seven areas church schools were over-subscribed and their matching county schools are under-subscribed. In another four areas the county schools are over-subscribed while the church schools were under-subscribed. In the remaining areas, thirteen matched county and church schools are over-subscribed and in one area both are under-subscribed. Unfortunately the picture is incomplete as nine of the ten church schools that are not paired with county schools are over-subscribed and comparable statistics for relevant county schools were unavailable.

Admissions policies for church primary schools while having some of the features of secondary schools' policies differ in important ways. One major difference is the emphasis on serving the local neighbourhood and local parishes.

Table 9 gives details of the admissions criteria for church primary schools.

Admissions Policies

TABLE 9: *Admissions criteria for church primary schools*

	Number of schools	Percentage
First priority to practising Anglican in parish, secondly, other Christians	9	(24.3)
First priority to siblings, secondly practising Anglicans in parish, thirdly, other Christians	10	(27.0)
First priority to practising Anglicans in parish, secondly, siblings	2	(5.4)
Equal priority to practising Anglicans and other Christians in locality, secondly, siblings	3	(8.1)
First priority to Church affiliation and children of other faiths	1	(2.7)
Open admissions policy	7*	(19.0)
Prepared to accept anyone who will participate in Christian life of school	5	(13.5)
Total	37	(100.0)

Note: Included in this category is one school where social reasons were given top priority.

Twenty-one (55 per cent) primary schools are over-subscribed and in these schools the admissions criteria are strictly adhered to.

Under-subscribed schools have open admissions policies where all children applying are offered places. One headteacher summed up the situation in the following way — 'Our school has always been an open house. There is no ban on children of other faiths or of no faith'. However, five under-subscribed schools accepted pupils if their parents agreed that the acceptance of a place for their child was tacit acceptance too of the Christian life of the school.

While one school in theory gave priority to Christians there were no Christian children in the school — 98 per cent of the pupils were Muslims and 2 per cent were Hindus and Sikhs.

Only three admissions policies refer explicitly to a criterion for children of other faiths. That is not to say they are excluded from primary schools, they are offered places under criteria covering proximity to school, parents who want their child to have a church school education or social and medical needs. Table 10 gives the details of the religious background of primary school pupils in the study.

Admissions policies in the majority of primary schools are linked closely to the needs of the neighbourhood. They are neighbourhood schools serving the local community and reflecting the cultural, religious and racial diversity of the neighbourhood in their pupil intake. Thirty-three (89 per cent) headteachers said their pupil intake reflected the neighbourhood composition. In fact, the majority of primary school teachers emphasize the importance of serving the local community. The proximity factor not only covers children living in the immediate neighbourhood or residents in the parish or surrounding parish but in

Faith, Culture and the Dual System

TABLE 10: Percentage distribution on religious backgrounds of pupils attending primary schools

Christians	Number	Percentage	Other faiths	Number	Percentage
Anglicans	1	(2.7)	1–9 per cent	16	(43.2)
All Christians majority C of E	3	(8.1)	10–19 per cent	5	(13.5)
90–99 per cent	10	(27.0)	20–29 per cent	1	(2.7)
80–89 per cent	2	(5.4)	50–59 per cent	2	(5.4)
70–79 per cent	1	(2.7)	60–69 per cent	1	(2.7)
60–69 per cent	1	(2.7)	100 per cent other faiths	1	(2.7)
50–59 per cent	1	(2.7)	No precise figures but other faiths in school	2	(5.4)
40–49 per cent	3	(8.1)			
30–39 per cent	2	(5.4)			
20–29 per cent	2	(5.4)	No pupil of other faiths	4	(10.9)
10–19 per cent	1	(2.7)			
Under 10 per cent	2	(5.4)	Information not given	5	(13.5)
Majority Christians — no precise figures	2	(5.4)	Total	37	(100.0)
No Christians	1	(2.7)			
Majority no religious affiliation	1	(2.7)			
No statistics provided	4	(10.9)			
Total	37	(100.0)			

many cases the proximity of parents' place of work in relation to the school. Out of the thirty-five schools supplying details, fourteen primary schools (35 per cent) serve their local parish only. A further twelve schools serve up to four parishes each. Six schools each serve between five and seven parishes. The remaining three schools serve eight, twelve and fifteen parishes respectively.

Many of these primary schools are situated in areas where there are large numbers of ethnic minority groups. One headteacher listed twenty-three countries of origin for his pupils. The religious diversity is reflected in the religious backgrounds: Anglicans, Methodists, Baptists, various Caribbean Pentecostals, non-practising Roman Catholics, Coptics, Rastafarians, Muslims, Hindus, Buddhists and Orthodox Jewish children. There are many similar examples of diversity found in primary schools.

At primary level, interviewing pupils, and in some cases, parents as well, is the exception to the rule. Only two headteachers interview parents and pupils and another three schools interview parents only before offering their child a place. In the remaining schools parents are invited to visit the schools and talk to the headteachers regarding the education of their children.

Two schools have devised a form which enable parents to invite a priest or minister to submit a personal recommendation for a place at the school.

Twenty (54 per cent) primary schools in the study were over-subscribed. In order to find out if headteachers agree in principle with the view that primary schools should be for children in the neighbourhood regardless of their background they were asked — do you think that admissions policies for church primary-aided schools should give priority to the children of the neighbourhood whatever their religious affiliation? Their replies show a discrepancy between what should happen in theory and what happens in practice. Nineteen teachers (52 per cent) said that priority should be given to local children, while twelve (32 per cent) said that priority should be given to children whose parents were practising members of the Church of England. Six teachers (16 per cent) were uncertain. Seven headteachers of under-subscribed schools said that admissions should be based on religious criteria whereas in practice they were operating open admissions policies.

Since the 1944 Education Act large numbers of all-age parish schools have become primary schools. As a result the Church of England's share in education is largest at primary school level where in 1984 just under 25 per cent of pupils were in C of E primary schools, whereas only 5 per cent of pupils were in C of E secondary schools. In some dioceses the imbalance of primary and secondary provision is very pronounced. In the London Diocese, for example, there are 139 voluntary-aided primary schools and seventeen voluntary-aided secondary schools.

The disproportionate number of church primary to secondary schools leads to situations where parents who wish their children to continue their education in a church school find that demand exceeds supply. When pupils apply for places in church secondary schools they are often presented with the fact that the Church of England secondary school intake is predominantly, if not entirely, Christian.

Today, church schools' admissions policies in over-subscribed situations are far removed from the policy adopted by the founders of the National Society. In their first annual report they dealt with the question of over-subscription in the following way — 'If more children should be recommended than can be admitted into the school, their names shall be put into a bag and as many as can be admitted drawn out'.[6]

In this chapter I have provided information on admissions policies for county and church schools and illustrated what are the given rules which assign children their places in these schools in a number of different contexts. Particular emphasis has been placed on the micro level of analysis and admissions policies have, therefore, been dealt with quite separately from effect on schools or indeed society.

We have seen that pupil admissions to county schools are a result of policy decisions which are determined on an area level by the LEA. County schools admit all pupils in a given area regardless of religion or culture. While variations in church schools' admissions policies are evident they are, nevertheless, concerned first and foremost with the Christian faith. Closely linked to the centrality of Christianity are the concepts of 'belonging' and 'practising'.

Many admissions policies in church primary schools (and to a lesser extent, church secondary schools) have been denominated by social, cultural and demographic changes in society. For under-subscribed schools there is little opportunity to be concerned only with children from Christian backgrounds. These schools have tended, some reluctantly, to come to terms with changes in the environment. For some, accommodation has been an instinctive reaction, adaptation the norm and compromises the order of the day. Admissions policies stressing Christian affiliation becomes untenable in certain situations. The boundaries for under-subscribed church schools become less and less discernible.

Notes

1. *Education Act 1980*, Section 6 (1).
2. *Education Act 1980*, Section 7 requires LEAs and governors of voluntary-aided and special agreement schools to make the necessary arrangements for parents to appeal if they are dissatisfied with an admissions decision.
3. *Notes for Guidance — Admission of Pupils* 81/5.
4. Statistics were quoted in school prospectus.
5. I mentioned in chapter 1 that the sample of church secondary schools represents 42.6 per cent of all Church of England secondary schools with voluntary aided status (excluding schools 'middle deemed secondary').
6. First annual report of the National Society for Promoting the Education of the Poor in the Principles of the Established Church 1812, p. 45.

Chapter 3

Admissions for Change

Admissions policies adopted by church schools highlight points of tension for both church and county schools. Tension manifests itself in different ways. County headteachers talked about areas which give rise to feelings of frustration and despondency — educational cuts, falling pupil rolls, teacher redundancies, curriculum contractions, school closures and amalgamations were all pressures that were being experienced by schools at the time of our research. In isolation these occurrences may be seen by many as inevitable, others will find them difficult to justify. However, what is significant is the way these changes are linked to the view that church schools are shielded from many of their effects. Church schools are seen in general as having far more control in shaping their own destinies.

While some of the areas of tension listed do display certain local elements especially where church schools are over-subscribed and the local county schools are under-subscribed schools that were distanced from such trends felt it was only a matter of time before the same pattern would start to emerge and they too would experience some of the pressures.

It is worth recalling that in the Inner London Education Authority where ten church schools in the study were not matched because of county school closures, amalgamations or pending amalgamations, not one Church of England voluntary-aided school had closed although one church secondary school had changed its voluntary-aided status to a voluntary-controlled status. In this case the governors retained control over religious education and all other powers rested with the local education authority.

The same local education authority compiled projected figures up to 1990 giving the pupil rolls for church and county secondary schools. In 1981 Church of England voluntary-aided secondary schools provided

Faith, Culture and the Dual System

for 17 per cent of the pupil population and county schools provided for 52 per cent. Unless Church of England schools share the effects of falling rolls, by 1990 the pupils in county schools would be reduced to 29 per cent while pupils in Church of England schools would account for 22 per cent of the pupil population. It is within this context that teachers in county schools argue that the effects of falling rolls must be shared by county and church schools alike.

In other areas where church and county schools are together experiencing the effects of falling rolls and educational cuts there is evidence of pulls and tensions. These schools in general, see themselves in competition for survival. Energies are channelled towards a search for survival strategies rather than being involved in a collective endeavour and responding as partners in education to the underlying changes in society.

Despite the tensions that exist between some church and county schools, seventeen (60 per cent) county headteachers considered their relationship with their local church schools as satisfactory while eleven (40 per cent) said their relationship was either unsatisfactory or 'nonexistent'. The main reasons given for unsatisfactory relationships are highlighted in the following sets of comments made by headteachers.

> We have an unsatisfactory relationship. The church school is far too exclusive, it is a school which has chosen to stand outside the local community and exercise its rights as a voluntary aided school.

> There is a problem because there is a public relationship and there is the reality of it all. They will not stop their piratical admissions policy. They are bussing children in ... It is naked academic and social selection.

> At the local level in terms of cooperation and dealing with pupil behaviour outside the school the relationship is good. At other levels the staff in this school have felt disquieted. If some church school children are expelled we usually have to take them because they live near the school. The staff here feel the poor neighbours because we don't have the same power levers as church schools. Also there is emotive feeling about their admissions policy and their intake.

Others referred to relationships as being one of 'intense rivalry' or the only link being one of 'competitors'.

Some ILEA county headteachers illustrate how their own intake of pupils is 'skewed' as a result of church schools' admissions policies. They describe the situation where a popular church secondary school is over-subscribed in bands 1 and 2 and can fill all the places in these two bands without difficulty. However, if the county school is affected by falling rolls it is possible for vacant places to remain in the top two bands. The more the county school is affected by falling rolls and unable to get its full quota in the top bands, the more unequal are the chances of achieving the same academic results in terms of public examination as the matching church schools. These schools will inevitably appear more 'successful' in terms of public examinations than the local county school.

Church schools frequently offer places to children outside the ILEA. Accordingly, these pupils are outside the banding arrangements. One headteacher points out, 'there is nothing to stop the church school accepting a higher proportion of band 1 children'. Another county headteacher said the church school 'poaches' his pupils. He explained that some parents who are unsuccessful in securing a place in a church school for their child put their name on a waiting list and when there is a vacant place the child is transferred to the church school. He remarked 'We lose some of our brightest kids in this way. Transfers never affect the troublesome ones'.

Thus, falling rolls and educational cuts have brought many aspects of the dual system into much sharper focus. Admissions policies are seen as 'protecting privileged interests'. Power and privilege are words that were frequently used by county headteachers in expressing their unsatisfactory relationships with church schools.

The autonomy of church schools concerning their admissions policies; their relative independence when compared with county schools; the ability of governors to frustrate the re-organization policies of local education authorities in a time of falling rolls, when combined, highlight the local power of church schools and at the same time illustrate the lack of local power for county school teachers. The 1944 Education Act which resulted in a settlement between state and churches was not concerned with providing 'privileges' for the churches but with providing a legal framework for education where the state and the churches could work together as partners. Today when the provisions laid down in the 1944 Act are interpreted as 'privileges', it is difficult not to come to the conclusion that in some instances these 'privileges' polarize church and county schools. County headteachers' comments give voice to the frustrations and tensions arising from church schools' admissions policies and the powers of their governing bodies.

Many church schools' admissions policies have evolved in response to immediate problems and pressures. Nowhere is this more apparent than in headteachers' replies to questions on when their admissions policies were last reviewed and their reasons given for the review. Thirty-four (89 per cent) secondary headteachers said that their admissions policies had been revised as a result of the 1980 Education Act.

The 1980 Education Act (section 8) which makes it compulsory for all schools to publish information about their school has had some unintended consequences for church schools. They must now give details of their admissions policies, the number of available places, arrangements to allow parents to express their preferences concerning the school for their child and arrangements for dissatisfied parents to appeal. Headteachers point out that as a result of the Act some children were now excluded who would have been offered a place before the Act came into effect. The Act has resulted in schools becoming 'more denominational in character' and their admissions procedure less flexible. Indeed, some schools did not have a clear policy statement on admissions prior to the Act. Headteachers' comments reveal that the group of parents who benefit most were those parents who claimed some allegiance to Chrisianity, no matter how tenuous the association. The form sent to the clergy to support a pupil's application has become more important since the Act as it provides more precise information for the Appeals Committee. Two primary school headteachers highlight the different effects of the Act for their schools.

> Prior to the 1980 Education Act we had a normal admissions policy which was rather airy-fairy but it did give me leeway to take a whole range of children. Then because of the 1980 Act the school had to draw up five points. These were based on the Act and on Diocesan advice. I do not like the admissions policy with its emphasis on Church affiliation. ... There is a danger that church schools can be just preaching to the converted. The Act has constrained not liberated schools.

Another said:

> Some governors prefer to leave certain things unstated leaving it to their discretion. The 1980 Act has taken away any room for discretion. The first year after the Act we had twenty-seven upheld appeals so now we spell out our admissions criteria in detail.

Others mentioned problems with the category 'families who are regular worshippers'. There are difficulties over the interpretation of the word 'regular'. Several appeals have hinged on this word.

The criteria covering 'special or medical reasons' also cause difficulties for another school. The headteacher commented that as a result of the 1980 Act he needs support from the borough in the form of a letter from the social worker or medical authority. Prior to this he could be more flexible under this category, for example . . . 'taking children from broken homes, on compassionate grounds, those in need of special pastoral care. Now I can't take some of those as I did in the past under this criteria. The group most affected now are the ethnic minority groups — they can't cope with all the formalities'.

The emphasis on parental preference stated in the 1980 Act has also been seen as beneficial for church schools (and, it seems, for the education authority) as one secondary headteacher explains in the statement produced below.

> One reason why we are keeping up our numbers in a time of falling rolls is that the Act has broken down educational boundaries. In fact the education authority benefits financially from out-borough children. We are getting children who are coming from further afield . . . We have always had some from outside but the numbers have increased since the 1980 Act.

While the same facility of accepting pupils from other LEAs is available to county schools in some education authorities, 'out County' intakes are seen by critics of church schools as their way of strengthening their position expecially when linked to the fact that governors of church schools are able to determine 'the operating capacity of the school'. Rogers argues 'Not only does this create an even more elitist admissions policy with church schools "poaching" from other areas, but it often gives the churches an impact on local educational affairs out of all proportion to their local support'.[1] It is interesting to ask whether the implementation of the 1980 Education Act has resulted in any way approximating the intentions of the legislators.

In 1981, twenty headteachers in Church of England secondary schools (the majority were headteachers of London schools) issued a statement (the Allington Statement) concerning the distinctive character of Church of England schools, their relationship with the Church of England and their county school neighbours. They question whether their autonomy 'is a help or hindrance' in their educational task. They express concern at the increasing criticism of church schools, both from inside and outside the church. Recognition is given to 'the need for church schools to be accountable to the church at large, as well as society as a whole' and suggest that there should be 'properly negotiated changes' in the autonomy of church schools.[2] These teachers proposed changes to reduce the powers in respect of individual church schools and so move towards a reduction of friction.

In their second statement issued a year later the Allington signatories stressed that 'all are at one' in their determination to see their schools 'united as the Church of England's educational arm in service of Christ and society'. To achieve this they envisage a close partnership in decision-making between governing bodies and dioceses, particularly in matters affecting church school provision. When headteachers in church secondary schools were asked by us whether they thought that church schools should be more accountable to the dioceses, only ten (26 per cent) said yes, fifteen (39 per cent) said no, and thirteen headteachers (34.9 per cent) were either uncertain or they had reservations. The following extracts illustrate the main reasons why headteachers were either reluctant or unwilling to surrender any powers to the diocesan education committees:

> I have reservations depending on how effective and how knowledgeable the diocese is. At the moment the governors would be reluctant to give up our autonomy and authority to a body that wasn't qualified to use it.
>
> It depends on the calibre of the diocesan officers themselves and also on the quality of advice they give ... In my experience you only take the advice if you respect the adviser. There has been the feeling that the professionalism of the board as far as experience and teachers are concerned, is somewhat less than the schools themselves.

There is little incentive to surrender autonomy when there is limited confidence in the expertise and structures of diocesan boards of education. On the other hand, there is little incentive for dioceses to make changes while their role remains an advisory one. The Allington Statement points out that this state of affairs could be overcome if there was a commitment from the schools 'to surrender negotiated areas of their autonomy as soon as agreed changes have been made in diocesan structures'.[3] Such collaborative action could bring church schools more in line with county schools where decisions on admissions policies and church school provision would be formulated on an area level, rather than on a local level.

The signatories of the Allington Statement believe that the time has come for the Church of England to work towards 'a coherent policy for its schools' which should be 'uniformly, adequately and sensitively administered both nationally and locally, in such a way as to encourage rather than stifle the individual school's enterprise'. Only then can the 'dual system' operate as a partnership between the state and the church — 'rather than between state and 5000 separate and autonomous governing bodies'.[4]

The question of whether the Church of England should have a central policy for all church schools was raised with headteachers in secondary schools. Their replies fell into three categories. Those who were against a central policy represented 45 per cent of the sample. Those who favoured a central policy without any reservation were a minority of eight teachers (21 per cent). The remaining thirteen headteachers (34 per cent) while thinking it could benefit church schools acknowledged some inherent difficulties.

Numerous headteachers called upon the Church of England to give church schools more support. Others questioned whether the Church favoured these schools at all. As one headteacher remarked 'If the Church of England believes in church schools then it should give more support. First of all it must make up its mind on the question of church schools — there is a certain degree of ambivalence'. Another said 'I want a more interested dialogue between the Church of England and their church schools. I want to know if it is totally committed to its schools or whether these schools are just remnants of the past'.

Headteachers who were against a central policy mentioned the diversity of church schools and their different environments with each school serving a different community. This view was expressed in the following way 'My reaction to this scheme, as always, is a local one. My chief nervousness about centralism is that church schools were founded to be local ... I don't need anyone to tell me how to apportion places'. Headteachers' answers were also coloured by whether their school had its own trust and was financially independent.

Critics of church schools have argued that parents choose a church school for academic rather than religious reasons.[5] One hundred and thirty-nine parents were asked to give their reasons for choosing a Church of England secondary school for their children. If parents gave more than one reason (thirty-six parents did) they were asked to say which they considered the most important. Their replies fell into four main categories — parents wanting a Church of England education; parents wanting a Christian education; parents who had chosen the school because of its academic reputation and, lastly, good discipline. Other reasons representing under seven per cent in each category included, proximity of school, its size, whether mixed or single sex school, friends at school, caring atmosphere, parental links, primary school links and 'nice kids'. Table 11 gives details of parents replies.

Faith, Culture and the Dual System

TABLE 11: Parents' reasons for selecting a Church of England secondary school

	First reason given Numbers	Percentage	Second reason given Numbers	Percentage
C of E education	36	(26)	8	(8)
Christian education	31	(22)	10	(10)
Academic reputation	32	(23)	29	(28)
Good discipline	10	(7)	21	(21)
Other	30	(22)	35	(33)
Total	139	(100)	103	(100)

A cross-check was carried out to validate the priority order of parents' replies. We were thus able to confirm the accuracy of the above table.

Column 1 is an accurate indicator of parents' main reason for choosing a church school. The Table indicates that just under half the parents interviewed (48 per cent) gave Christian education (this figure includes C of E education) as top priority in their choice of school. Selecting a school for its academic reputation is the main consideration for just under a quarter of the sample of parents (23 per cent). When parents' first and second reasons are combined the percentage of parents who give reasons concerning the academic reputation of the school increases to 44 per cent. While it would be surprising if parents were not concerned about the academic reputation this statistic strongly indicates that the academic reputation of the school was of central importance for just under half of all the parents interviewed.

Sixty parents had considered a county school education before deciding on a church school. Seventeen of these parents after considering the county school selected the church school because its academic reputation was better. This finding reinforces the fact that some parents do choose a school purely on its academic reputation.

A major element in discussions of church schools concerns their potentially divisive nature.[6] Most of this concern has been directed at admissions policies and practices. Rogers points to what he sees as an imbalance that affects local county schools.

> Admitting children on religious grounds inevitably excludes children of other faiths or none. In a multiethnic area this can and does create an unfortunate imbalance between local schools, with near all-white church schools and blacker than usual county schools.[7]

While there is undoubtedly some truth in Rogers' statement for some schools it is however too generalized. It simplifies what is indeed a complex area — it tends to distort what is a many faceted situation into a

Admissions for Change

uniform coherent one. Furthermore, it masks the type of divisiveness that can occur. For Green some church schools' policies could be criticized individually but they did not justify the condemnation of all admissions policies.

> ... there is no reason for laying down a blanket criticism and to attack the entire dual system. Such a stance may provide good 'copy' for the media but it does not provide the basis for a mature, fair analysis upon which sensible judgment can be made.
>
> Fair, genuine, constructive criticism of the Dual System is welcome. But prejudice, political opportunism, emotive language and ill-founded generalizations are unhelpful.[8]

There are two important points at issue in Rogers' statement. Firstly, that any imbalance that may occur is only one way (affecting county schools with a preponderance of black pupils) and secondly, the assumed link between religion and colour. It does not necessarily follow that black means non-Christian. Clearly, over-subscribed church schools which give first priority to children of Anglican parents and secondly, to those of other christian traditions and who fill all their places on these criteria alone, must face the accusation that their admissions policies exclude children of other faiths if their schools are situated in multifaith areas. Their admissions policies are implicitly and explicitly stating that their schools are for Christians. As such these admissions policies have the effect of causing the imbalance referred to by Rogers if they are situated in a multifaith areas.

On the other hand, over-subscribed schools using the same criteria which are situated in areas where there are a large number of West Indian families will offer places to these children if they are Christians (as indeed the majority of West Indians are). This too can have the effect of causing an imbalance where church schools have a higher percentage of black pupils than the local county schools. The reason for this is straightforward, it is not a colour criterion that is employed but a religious criterion.

There is no evidence from our research to suggest that church schools exclude black Christians. This finding confirms the results of a limited study carried out by the Runnymede Trust which looked at the admissions policies in eight Anglican and seven Roman Catholic schools and twenty church and county primary schools.[9]

Green, in recognizing that the majority of church secondary schools in London give first priority for admission to children of Anglican parents and secondly to those of the main Christian traditions, points to

39

the need for a close examination of these policies because church schools may be unwittingly stumbling towards the creation of totally Christian, and even denominational schools. They are on the brink of breaking with tradition without foreseeing the consequences'.[10]

A group of Christians committed to racial justice and combating racism and fascism issued a pamphlet which raised a number of issues facing church schools in a multifaith society. They too voiced their concern over pupil admission:

> *Some* church schools emphasize their Christian basis and thereby either exclude, in practice, children of other faiths thus becoming unrepresentative of their neighbourhood. Thus in *some* areas church schools have become white enclaves using religion as a means of discrimination.[11]

This statement was included in the interview schedule for headteachers in church secondary schools and they were asked to express their views. Eleven teachers (29 per cent) said that they tried not to let this statement be true for their school but there are difficulties. Another eight (21 per cent) said that it did not represent what is happening in their schools. Seven headteachers (18 per cent) agreed that the statement was true and could be applied to their schools. They said that Christian parents were entitled to a church school education for their children. Headteachers who represent the largest group (32 per cent), were either unable to answer the question, were reluctant to comment or had no firm views. For these headteachers there was no real questioning of such a controversial statement.

Every effort was made to collect statistics on the ethnic backgrounds of pupils from headteachers. Problems were encountered in obtaining information of this nature. The distinction between ethnic groups and racial groups was often blurred.[12] Some headteachers said they did not 'head count', others did not collect comprehensive statistics. While others said 'it is difficult to tell with some what their background is' other teachers use the criteria of colour, language or geographical origin. English as a second language (ESL) provision is sometimes used as an indicator. There are obvious problems with language indicators, for a significant number of ethnic minority groups English is their prime language. Some headteachers could say how many nationalities were represented in the school — but they could not always specify what percentage of the pupil population they accounted for.

Headteachers in church schools are more likely to have a clearer idea of the different faiths rather than the number of ethnic groups. With county school headteachers the reverse is often true. They are

Admissions for Change

more likely to provide information on the different ethnic groups but have greater difficulty in providing information as to the religious affiliation of pupils. Another difficulty encountered in church schools is the reply 'They are all Christians' — this did not however provide information on the percentage of black Christians without further questioning.

All LEAs involved in the research were asked if they collected statistics on the ethnic composition of pupils in their authority and, if they did, whether they would be willing to provide the relevant statistics for schools in the study. These statistics were provided for seventeen county schools (representing 61 per cent of the county school sample) twenty-four church secondary schools (63 per cent of sample) and twenty-one primary schools (57 per cent of sample).[13]

Looking at the statistics relating to the ethnic backgrounds of pupil composition in ten inner London church secondary schools and their matched county and primary schools it is possible to draw some firm conclusions.[14] The comparative statistics for county and church secondary schools will be discussed first. Four out of ten church schools have a higher percentage of English, Scots, Welsh and Irish pupils than their paired county schools — the differences range from 3 to 20 per cent. Seven out of ten church schools have a higher percentage of Caribbean pupils than the corresponding county schools. The differences range from 5 to 35 per cent.

On the other hand, all ten London county schools have a higher percentage of pupils in the categories Bangladeshi, Indian, Pakistan, than their matching church schools. The statistics show very clearly that there is greater diversity to be found in county schools in terms of the nationalities of their pupils. It is clear from these statistics that at secondary level, ethnic minority pupils are, in the main, concentrated in county schools. The degree of concentration is greatest among Asian pupils. On the other hand, when the statistics for the two categories 'English, Scots, Welsh and Irish' and 'Caribbean' are combined they account for between 65 and 89 per cent of the pupil population in nine of the ten church secondary schools.

Turning to look at some of the differences in the pupil composition in church primary and secondary schools some interesting observations can be made. Combining the statistics in table 1 of Appendix 2, fourteen out of eighteen primary schools have a smaller percentage of English, Scots, Welsh and Irish pupils than the matched church secondary schools. When the statistics for the categories 'Afro-Asian, Bangladeshi, Indian and Pakistan are combined eleven primary schools have a higher percentage of pupils in these groups. In three paired schools, however, there was no significant difference and four secondary schools had more. On the other hand, eleven church secondary schools have a higher percentage of Caribbean pupils than in the corresponding primary schools. These differences vary from 2 to 29 per cent.

These statistics suggest that the backgrounds of pupils in church primary schools are more likely to resemble the diversity to be found in county schools. Only two outer London boroughs provided statistics on ethnic composition of pupils. In one borough there was no significant difference in the ethnic composition of pupils. However, in the second London borough white pupils accounted for 82 per cent in the county schools and 100 per cent in the matched church secondary school.

Admissions policies for church secondary schools which stress Christian related criteria have the effect of restricting the possibility of cultural and religious diversity within the school environment. While these schools provide for diversity among Christian children from different cultural and racial groups there is less opportunity for pupils to interact with children from other faiths and cultures. Thus diversity and the potential for interaction is more likely to be found in church primary schools, where admissions policies are, to a far greater extent, more open.

The research found notable differences between schools in inner London and schools in the north-west region and the West Midlands. In the ILEA schools, one in six children speak English as a second language and 147 languages are spoken by pupils. The most common languages represented in these schools are Bengali, Gujerati, Urdu, Punjabi, Chinese, Greek, Spanish, Italian, French, Portuguese, Arabic and Turkish.[15] As a result there is greater cultural diversity to be found in London schools than in the schools we visited in the north-west region and the West Midlands. Headteachers in the north-west region and the West Midlands commented on London schools as being essentially multicultural in the pupil intake while their schools 'are really bi-cultural, indigenous and Asian'. While such an interpretation is simplistic in assuming there is only one culture to be found among the 'indigenous British' and one culture among Asians, the point they were making was that ethnic groups of Asian origin form a sizeable and significant percentage of the pupil population. These headteachers tended to provide statistics using these two categories, White and Asian, which therefore required a deeper probing on our part.

An LEA spokesman in the north-west region illustrated how two quite different admissions policies can have the same effect on pupil composition in schools and result in an absence of ethnic minority children in both the church and its matching county school. On the one hand the county school draws its pupils from a very tight catchment area which does not contain significant numbers of ethnic minority groups. Although areas near the school but outside the catchment area were heavily populated with families of Asian origin there were none in the school. The church secondary school's catchment area covered the entire metropolitan borough. It could draw from areas with large numbers of ethnic minority groups but the education officer said 'ethnic minority groups are not offered a place because of the school's preference for Christian affiliation. Indeed these groups are unlikely to apply'.

For the above schools' matched Church of England primary school 50 per cent of the pupils are Muslims. None of these pupils go to the church secondary school. This creates problems for the headteacher in the primary school in terms of explaining why the ethnic minority groups are acceptable in the primary school but not in the secondary school. It is impossible for Muslims to qualify for admission unless the level of application drops to below 240. This secondary school used to be a direct grant grammar school — 'Its image in the eyes of parents as well as its image as a church school among Anglicans is still a high academic image. This school must be parents' first preference otherwise their child will not get in'.

The imbalance between primary and secondary church school provision in many areas gives rise to considerable concern among primary headteachers. When parents apply for places at secondary schools they are frequently presented with the fact that the Church of England secondary school is predominantly, if not entirely, for Christians.

In another LEA in the north-west region similar patterns were found. A church secondary school situated in an inner city area admits no children from ethnic minority groups (of non-Christian faiths unless they come into the sixth-form which has a more open entrance policy). Yet the matching county school has a substantial number and employs several section II teachers.

The matching church junior school has pupils from twelve families of ethnic origin. In another church primary school which was nearby (and not included in the study) pupils from ethnic minority groups make up 60 per cent of the pupil population. This school serves an area of older terraced property built at the time of the industrial revolution and where immigrants have now settled.

In the West Midlands all three church secondary schools and their matching county schools were situated in areas with substantial numbers of ethnic groups, the majority originating from India, Bangladesh and

Faith, Culture and the Dual System

Pakistan. In these schools a familar pattern emerged. Pupils of Asian origin account for a higher percentage of the school population in county schools than they do in church secondary schools. In some areas the differences are very marked. In one church secondary school the statistics show that 93 per cent of pupils are white whereas in the matched county school, 21 per cent of the pupils are white. The church primary school had an even smaller percentage of white pupils (16.7 per cent). It is in this type of situation that critics of church schools have labelled them as 'White enclaves'.[16]

Turning to look at the pupil composition for schools in the north-west region, we found that in two out of three areas where statistics were provided, county schools had a much smaller percentage of white pupils. In one county school white pupils accounted for 22 per cent and pupils of African, Indian, Bangladesh and Pakistan origins accounted for 78 per cent of all pupils. Whereas for the matching church school, white pupils accounted for 93 per cent of all pupils. In the second county school pupils of African, Indian, Bangladesh and Pakistan origins accounted for 93 per cent and white pupils 3 per cent of all pupils. In the matching church school white pupils accounted for 50 per cent.

Our research shows generally that where there is a large concentration of Asian families their presence will not be reflected in the nearby church secondary school (unless they are Christians) to the same extent as the local county school. Indeed, some popular church secondary schools, as we have seen, do not reflect these groups at all. In the areas visited during the research the majority of Asians were Muslims with Hindus and Sikhs in smaller numbers. The reason why they were either under-represented or not represented at all in certain church secondary schools is summed up by a headteacher — 'Our church-affiliated criteria would tend to keep them out anyway'. Such admissions policies have the effect of reinforcing divisions along religious lines within the local community as the following extracts illustrate:

> The neighbourhood contains Asians in good numbers, but we usually have Asians who have a Christian faith of some sort. We do not take Muslims therefore Pakistanis don't apply.
>
> This is the ninth largest Asian population in the country ... There are about forty-seven Anglican parishes ... Only about twenty youngsters are within walking distance of the school. The school admits purely on Church of England affiliation.

In general, it is true to say the church primary schools will be representative of the neighbourhood in terms of their pupil intake and

Admissions for Change

so they tend to reflect relevant cultural and religious concerns.

In summing up the effects of admissions policies for his school and the area as a whole, one primary headteacher commented: 'We have black, white and brown pupils. The faiths they represent are Christian, Muslim, Hindu and Sikh. There's also a significant vocal element who are Rastafarians. We are unusual in this area in that we are so mixed. The other schools are either predominantly Asian, dominantly white, for example, the Roman Catholic school, or white and West Indian with no Asians the C of E secondary school'.

There are exceptions to be found in primary schools where priority is given to Anglicans and Christians. These are popular, over-subscribed schools accepting children from long distances and as such they are not neighbourhood schools. As one primary teacher explains — 'We are certainly not a neighbourhood school. We get children from all over the borough and some from outside ... Many of the children need transport to get here. Few can actually walk to the school. The parents who actually transport their children here are interested in their children's education and, in general, they are middle class'.

It would appear from our study that not all headteachers recognize either the extent of the effects, or the full implications of their own admissions policies. Some headteachers were self-questioning but were at the same time content to reflect a comfortable and apparently complacent view, as the following headteacher shows in her discussion on pupil admissions:

> Yes, I must admit our admissions policy does cause tension with our county neighbours and perhaps we should look at it again. In the end, however, I am only concerned with the success of our school.

Again, in another situation, no trace of discomfort is apparent from another headteacher's remarks:

> If we abandon our C of E priority and become a neighbourhood school we would fill up with Asians. If this happened, I would want to abandon it as a church school.

Even so, it is noteworthy that other teachers did express concern that their admissions policies were in danger of creating 'holy huddles', 'monastic settlements' or giving the impression of 'a chosen people's image'.

The difficulties surrounding the accusation of some church schools as 'White enclaves' could, in some areas, be overcome by adopting an admissions policy that admits pupils on the basis of 'foundation and non-foundation' places. The National Society, in its guidelines on admissions policies, recommends that governors give careful consideration to the possibility of devizing an admissions application form which would enable parents to apply for 'a particular class of place in the school rather than a place in general'.[17] The National Society suggests that where governors see the role of the school as both a service to the wider community and a service to the 'narrower church-going sector' available places in the school could be divided into a number of foundation places and non-foundation places. The foundation places would be given to pupils with Anglican connections. The 'non-foundation' places would be available for children applying for a place who did not have church connections. The proportion of non-foundation places available must not be sub-divided in such a way as to give rise to a quota system. They point out that 'The Commission for Racial Equality considers that an allocation of places to racial groups in strict numerical terms could be illegal. An admissions policy based on religious grounds is in the Commission's opinion not illegal provided that when governors fail to admit a pupil that refusal can be justified on religious grounds or on non-racial grounds'.

Headteachers in church secondary schools were asked to give their views on the National Society's suggestion of allocating foundation and non-foundation places. Twenty-three (61 per cent) thought it was a good idea although six teachers thought it would be difficult to administer. One school has already decided to adopt the scheme and in another two schools discussions were taking place to consider the possibility of offering places based on the two categories. Eleven (29 per cent) found the National Society's suggestion unacceptable and four teachers (10 per cent) were not sure.

Headteachers in favour of the scheme brought different perspectives to the issues. The following quotations extracted from extended readings of discussions capture some of the variety to be found in their replies:

> I agree with the suggestion. Our original foundation was set up to instruct pupils in the christian faith, not reinforce/teach those already so instructed.

No doubt this headteacher's views may well cause some educationalists a headache. Another headteacher, while agreeing, pointed out that the scheme did not apply to his school:

> This scheme does not apply to our school. It is devised for schools where admissions criteria are divisive. We are unusual. I

Admissions for Change

would not want a monastic settlement of committed Christians. If we were, I would welcome the scheme.

Yet another headteacher point out:

> The whole purpose of Christianity is to go out to all children. Church schools should not close their doors to those that do not attend church. This is opposed to Christian teaching.

Another headteacher illustrated how children of other faiths can be at a disadvantage in a church school:

> In principle I agree and in practice it is possible. Some staff feel that because of the heavy over-subscription in bands 1 and 2 any Hindus and Muslims admitted will come in on band 3. Quite a number of staff feel that some children i.e. Hindus and Muslims are therefore disadvantaged by the rules and would like innovation.

This headteacher would like to reserve places for children from disadvantaged religious groups and they would be given priority. He did say he would not include Roman Catholics in this group because they have their own schools.

This is an appropriate point at which to transfer the discussion to another area of concern which also relates to admissions practice. In county schools children from ethnic minority groups will be found throughout all three ability groups. Where the banding system operates, headteachers in under-subscribed church schools mentioned that pupils without church connections and belonging to other faiths are able to get a place in band 3 only. Headteachers need to look at the consequences of these children not being represented in top ability bands and over-represented in low ability groups as a direct result of the school's admissions policy. Over-representation of other faiths in low attainment groups raises serious questions concerning the self-image of these children.

Headteachers who were opposed to the whole idea of foundation and non-foundation places did so for the following reasons:

(a) It cannot be right to refuse children of practising Anglican parents to admit others.
(b) No, I wouldn't accept it. It will be taking away from church schools a special role in life. I think you have got to look at what church schools are set up for. The Christian nature of the school would be diluted. Church schools are there for Christian pupils.

47

Faith, Culture and the Dual System

The headteachers were also concerned with the reactions of parents:

> If you have a school and it is over-subscribed by practising Christian parents and pupils, if you say 40 per cent can't come because of a deliberate policy of foundation and non-foundation places then Christian parents would be aggrieved. How can you justify turning down Christians for a few Muslims?
>
> The congregations of this deanery pay for the upkeep of this school. It would be difficult to justify keeping their children out.

Another headteacher, while against the scheme, made the following statement:

> It does not apply to us. If you look at us we take in ninety boys who will all have normal church connections. We are trying to preserve the faith of forty and build on a rather pathetic knowledge of another fifty. This is hard enough without taking in atheists and doing something for them. The spiritual life of the nation would not be enhanced by taking more in this catchment area.

In addition, others stressed that they were serving parishioners rather than the local community and that they were not neighbourhood schools.

These extracts from extended recorded discussions illustrate the divergent views that exist about the nature and purpose of church schools. Any question that is posed concerning admissions to church schools and potential areas for change highlights a basic divide that exists between those who see church schools for Christians, and in a minority of cases, for Anglicans only and those who see church schools in service of the nation's children. Closely allied to this view is the underlying assumption that they are not neighbourhood schools. It must also be said that the term 'neighbourhood school' is often used in an ill-defined way and is capable of use in a variety of ways. Nevertheless, it must be recorded that given the different reactions of headteachers, there is a fundamental view shared by all concerning the religious underpinning of church schools: all headteachers are united in providing education within a Christian environment. Church schools are seen as providing a distinctively Christian contribution to education.

In a Green Paper issued by the National Society the question of admissions to church schools is discussed at length. It states that 'admissions policies that are weighted in favour of a *single* criterion (such as a place of residence or religious affiliation) are likely to produce inequalities in the system and should be avoided'.[18] Later in the paper it goes on to say, 'The governing body of a Church of England aided school which insists on operating admissions almost entirely by means of the simple criterion of the family's attendance at worship is forgetting the general service to the nation's children that has always formed one of the twin aims of church schools'.[19] Furthermore, it points out that the undifferentiated twin aims which the Church of England has applied to its schools must continue today. School must be *'Both service to the general education of the nation* and *education in the Christian faith'*.[20] And yet our research has shown that 45 per cent of the sample fill all their places on church-related criteria and so for these schools the concept of church-relatedness is central.

We have seen that two secondary schools consider that they have no responsibility beyond that of the Anglican community while 48 per cent of the sample enlarge their responsibility to cover the Christian community which can be interpreted as 'a fellowship of denominational interests'.

The National Society's foundation and non-foundation scheme offers schools a framework where the historic twin aims can be reflected. Some headteachers, especially in under-subscribed schools, point out that their schools were in effect allocating foundation and non-foundation places although not stated explicitly in their published admissions policies. If the scheme were to be adopted after careful discussion and consideration by governors, staff and those involved locally, and subsequently clearly stated in published admissions policy, progress would be as a result of internally initiated change (although external forces cannot be excluded). Schools could thus maintain the integrity of historic aims without the need for fragmented pragmatic responses.

Admissions policies with built-in provision of foundation and non-foundation places would allow church schools to open their doors to the nation rather than say you can come providing there are no Christians wanting a place. An initiative which is confined to under-subscribed schools would be described with some justice as 'just tinkering with the system' or 'tokenism'. However, many headteachers in church schools both under-subscribed, as well as over-subscribed, said that parents from other faiths did not apply for places for their children. This could be due to the fact that only a minority of church primary and secondary schools explicitly mention criteria for children of other faiths in their admissions policies. A commitment to offering foundation and non-foundation places would avoid the situation where admissions policies are adapted merely to meet the forces of supply and demand. A headteacher's comments illustrate this point:

Faith, Culture and the Dual System

> These criteria are used exactly but they do need careful reading. They are often misquoted by parents. What they are actually saying is that you probably won't get in unless you go to church in a year when the church school is very over-subscribed. If we have a lot of competition then the emphasis is on church priority.

Admissions policies that are restructured in such a way could dismantle some but by no means all of the barriers that exist between church schools and their neighbourhoods. Clearly, any change in admissions policy that allows for a more varied intake is likely to stimulate change in other areas and this will entail careful examination of existing school policies and practices.

The substantial presence of other faiths in our society presents a radically new challenge for church schools. While there are no accurate statistics for members of faiths other than Christianity, community figures show that there are 1,500,000 Muslims in Britain, 412,000 Jews, 400,000 Hindus and 200,000 Sikhs; an estimated figure for Buddhists is put at 100,000.[21] Within the Church of England there is a recognition of these changes and evidence to show that important questions are being raised by those responsible for church school education on national, area, and local levels. The General Synod has called for an appropriate education programme to reflect the changes that have occurred. The National Society's Green Paper poses the question 'To whom does the Church of England school extend Christ's welcome?' Green published an occasional paper with the title 'What are church schools for' and the authors of the Allington Statement ask 'for which children'?

These questions require a thorough re-examination of the church school's responsibility with regard to those of other faiths and belief systems. There is the challenge of how the church itself can adjust and continue to maintain the central Christian tradition which the church school has contributed to education. The tension between continuity and the need to respond to the changing circumstances is ever-present. Rigid structures act as barriers to change, while a lack of structures or boundaries results in ambiguity and loss of any identifiable prime intention. David Martin illustrates how 'religious thinking' gains colour and meaning from its relationship with the total environment and an awareness of its ever changing nature.

> To move through an environment in such a way is to sense what range it allows and what range it forbids, to recognize gradually

what is an alien intrusion and what is a subtle and unexpected congruence.[22]

The National Society's Green Paper questions 'whether the Church of England should stand up for its historic share in education, simply by defending the status quo. Perhaps it should instead return to its historic role as *pioneer* and seek those points within the education service where new initiatives are required'.[23]

The question of relations between Christians and other faiths is of crucial importance and it provides the context for new initiatives. As an educational institution the church school is uniquely placed to treat the faith dimension seriously. The Board for Mission and Unity draws attention to the fact that Christians have in common with those of other faiths 'an awareness of and a search for, "the Other", "the ground of all being", though they use very different language, symbols and imagery to express it. This is a powerful witness to draw those of different faiths nearer to each other. Together they can challenge contemporary life-styles in the West, largely secularist in attitude, with its emphasis upon material goods and values'.[24] In a unique way the church school provides for children, both a private and a public acknowledgement of 'other worldly' values and realities. It has the potential to be inclusive of a variety of world faith perspectives even though at the present time it largely adopts an exclusive stance.

Bishop Newbigin while not disparaging the fact that scholars of different faiths meet in a formal way for dialogue, points out that 'the fact that we have to arrange such meetings may be a sympton of the fact that we are failing in the more elementary matter of day-to-day conversation with our neighbours of other faiths'.[25]

The British Council of Churches outlines four principles for dialogue which have the support of the General Synod of the Church of England. Firstly, dialogue takes place between people. Secondly, dialogue relies upon 'mutual understanding and mutual trust'. Thirdly, 'dialogue makes it possible to share in service to the community', and fourthly, for Christians 'dialogue becomes the medium of authentic witness'.[26] Clearly, the church school can provide a meeting place for meaningful dialogue between Christians and those of other faiths.

This chapter has been concerned with contributing to the debate on church schools by providing a reliable and empirically valid portrayal on what is happening concerning their admissions policies. A wider educational context was provided by county headteacher comment and criticism.

Faith, Culture and the Dual System

Existing admissions policies for church schools are far removed from a once coherent scheme of thought and action. Many schools now grasp at fragments of the scheme without recognizing the context in which they find themselves today. We have seen that admissions policies in many popular over-subscribed schools are designed with exclusive precision. They draw clear boundaries in order to designate who shall or shall not avail of a church school education. Schools using church affiliation criteria, make primary what is in effect a principle of exclusiveness. In addition, that which has acquired legitimacy from the past is seen as relevant, while changes in society today seem of less importance to the primary intention of responding to the needs of the worshipping community. These schools appeal to the principle of entitlement.

A minority of over-subscribed schools have, on the other hand, been able to keep to the forefront their inherited role which the Church of England saw as two-fold — providing for the needs of the nation in general and for the needs of Anglican children in particular.

Notes

1. ROGERS, R. (1981) 'Denominational schooling', *Multiracial Education*, 10, 1, p. 28.
2. *The Allington Statement*, p. 2. Also published in ILEA *Contact*, 16 October, 1981.
3. Allington — One Year On, p. 3.
4. *Ibid.* page 2.
5. 'Dual system end it or mend it,' *Teaching London Kids*. nos. 14, 16 and 17.
6. The dual system of voluntary and county schools, p. 8, Socialist Education Discussion Document.
7. ROGERS, R. (1981) *op. cit.*, p. 28.
8. GREEN, R. (1981) *A Personal View of the Church of England Inner and Greater London Schools*, London, London and Southwark Boards of Education.
9. DUMMETT, A. and MCNEAL, J. (1981) *Race and Church Schools*, London, Runnymede Trust.
10. GREEN, R. *What are Church Schools For?*, An occasional paper issued by the Schools Division, London and Southwark Boards of Education.
11. *Christians Against Racism and Facism*, Issues in the 80s.
12. WALLMAN, S. (1978) 'Race relations or ethnic relations', *New Community* VI, 3, summer. The article outlines the complexity of the terms 'race' and 'ethnicity' and points to the confusion when they are used interchangeably. In addition, she points out that neither 'ethnic' nor 'racial'

Admissions for Change

boundaries are 'consistently drawn in the same place and the meaning ascribed to either of the differences varies in different situations'.

13 Statistics are given in appendix 2.
14 Statistics for pupils in London schools are more detailed than those provided for the rest of England. Information was provided for a county school that was matched with a church secondary school but interviews with headteachers and religious education teachers did not take place.
15 Statistics taken from ILEA secondary schools.
16 This term is used by the authors of the Christians Against Racism and Fascism pamphlet.
17 *Admission of Pupils*, National Society, notes for Guidance, 81/5.
18 A *Future in Partnership*, 9.47, a Green paper for discussion published by the National Society (Church of England) for Promoting Religious Education 1984.
19 *Ibid*. p. 85.
20 *Ibid*. p. 97.
21 *Relations with People of Other Faiths*, p. 2, Guidelines for Dialogue in Britain, The British Council of Churches, Revised Edition 1983.
22 MARTIN, D. (1980) 'The breaking of the image', in A *Sociology of Christian Theory and Practice*, London, Basil Blackwell, p. 155.
23 A *Future in Partnership*, *op. cit.*, p. 54.
24 Board for Mission and Unity of the General Synod of the Church of England (1984) *Towards a Theology for Inter-Faith Dialogue*, London, C10 Publishing, p. 6.
25 Bishop Newbigin (1977) *Christian Witness in a Plural Society*, British Council of Churches, p. 18.
26 BCC *op. cit.*, p. 18, The BCC sees the four principles outlined as having specific relevance for church schools.

Chapter 4

Aspects of Diversity

The features of the dual system outlined in chapter I facilitate church schools with a voluntary-aided status to retain their relative independence. In addition to the right of governing bodies to develop their own pupil admissions policies another major area of their independence concerns the appointment of teaching staff. The power of governing bodies to appoint staff is seen as an important means of enabling church schools to continue to fulfil the intentions of Trust Deeds. As Trustee, the governing body acts as the guardian of the school's tradition. It specifies what those intentions are and its policies and practices are constructed in such a way as to perpetuate the wishes of the founders.

Twenty-six (68 per cent) headteachers of church secondary schools and twenty-two (59 per cent) in primary schools said that for their church schools the prime intention is to transmit the Christian faith and values in accordance with the principles/doctrines of the Church of England. For another four (11 per cent) headteachers of secondary schools and one primary headteacher their schools were founded to provide a Christian education which was not necessarily linked to the Church of England. The remaining headteachers were unable to comment on the Trust Deeds for their schools. It is noteworthy that the prospectuses for these schools classified them as Church of England schools. Clearly, for church schools with ancient foundations the founders would not have conceived of establishing a school with any other objectives.

It was evident from our discussions with governors and headteachers that governing bodies in appointing staff look for teachers who are best equipped to continue the tradition entrusted to their keeping.

In general, governors in appointing staff give first preference to applicants who are members of the Church of England, and secondly to teachers belonging to other Christian traditions. Indeed, many

TABLE 12: Percentage of teachers in church schools who are members of the Church of England

	Secondary schools	Primary schools
	Number (%)	Number (%)
All Church of England	–	2 (5.4)
80–89 per cent	5 (13.1)	7 (18.4)
70–79 per cent	5 (13.1)	6 (16.2)
60–69 per cent	3 (8.0)	4 (10.8)
50–59 per cent	4 (10.5)	–
40–49 per cent	3 (8.0)	5 (13.2)
20–29 per cent	2 (5.2)	3 (8.1)
Majority Church of England	6 (15.8)	2 (5.4)
Majority Christians	10 (26.3)	8 (21.6)
Don't know	–	–
Total	38 (100.0)	37 (100.0)

governing bodies when advertising a teaching post specify 'a communicant of the Church of England preferred'. Others specify 'Christians preferred'.

Headteachers were asked to provide details of the number of teachers who were members of the Church of England. This information is provided in table 12.

Table 12 shows that in just under half (45 per cent) of the secondary schools over 50 per cent of the teachers are members of the Church of England. This figure is higher for primary schools at 51 per cent.

Only four (11 per cent) secondary and two (5 per cent) primary headteachers said that all the teachers in their schools were Christians. In another twenty-seven (71 per cent) secondary and thirty (81 per cent) primary schools Christian teachers accounted for over 70 per cent of the teaching staff. It is evident that the ideal of a Christian staff is far removed from the everyday reality. Headteachers often pointed out that the religious stances of teachers ranged from committed Christians to agnostics and atheists.

In situations where non-Christians are appointed they are generally required to confirm that they are in sympathy with the religious aims and values of the school. Furthermore, at interviews for staff appointments, applicants are asked not only if they are in sympathy with the aims and values of the school but whether they are willing to participate in the full life of the school, for example, school worship. The point was made frequently that the school is more likely to achieve its aims if there is a consensus among the teaching staff as to those aims.

There were two exceptions where headteachers in secondary

Aspects of Diversity

schools said the religious affiliation of teachers was not of primary importance:

> The majority of the staff were appointed when it was a grammar school which admitted on a selective basis and these staff were appointed on academic ability rather than religious affiliation. I haven't varied this very much in my appointments. This might be very different to other Church of England schools.

In the second school the governors said 'we are looking for the best subject teacher and the first thing is his qualifications. If he is a Christian, it is a bonus.'

Headteachers were asked whether constitutionally their governing bodies could appoint teachers of other faiths. Seventeen (46 per cent) primary headteachers and thirty-three (87 per cent) secondary headteachers said that their governors could appoint members of other religious groups. The remaining teachers were not sure if this was the case.

In twelve (32 per cent) secondary and five (14 per cent) primary schools there are members of other faiths on the teaching staff. However, the numbers involved are very small. In all but one primary school they account for one member of the staff and in the remaining school two teachers of non-Christian faiths are employed. Six of the twelve secondary schools employed Jewish teachers (in one of these schools three Hindus are members of the teaching staff). In another two there is respectively one Hindu one Muslim and member of staff.

One of the main reasons given for the absence of teachers of other faiths is that the schools receive very few applications from these teachers. Clearly, the stipulation 'Christians preferred' acts as a deterrent for non-Christian teachers.

Primary headteachers discussed a major difficulty which they envisaged in employing teachers of other faiths which was concerned with religious education. As religious education in the majority of primary schools is integrated, teachers of other faiths would be required to teach the Christian faith. Not only did headteachers express their doubts about whether these teachers would have the expertise to teach Christianity but they were not sure whether Hindu, Sikh or Muslim teachers would want to teach Christianity which is what the school would want them to do. A primary headteacher recalled a situation where an atheist teacher was asked to teach pupils Christmas carols and the teacher was reluctant to do so and he wondered if teachers of other faiths would respond in a similar way.

Appointing staff who 'are in sympathy with the aims of the school is one of the main ways in which headteachers can maintain the school ethos. As one headteacher commented:

> The governors would not appoint anybody who is anti-Christian. They want teachers who are sympathetic to the Christian faith. This is because they would destroy the ethos of the school.

Contradictions inherent in current staff recruitment policies are demonstrated in the following headteacher's comment:

> In the last few years we have been putting 'Christians preferred' and getting them. But some of my best staff are agnostic and some of my worst teachers are Christian.

A pragmatic approach to teacher appointments was evident in some headteachers' replies when they discussed the appointment of non-Christian teachers.

A primary headteacher in distinguishing between permanent and temporary staff said:

> We have teachers of other faiths on the staff as they have been the best teachers available at the time. We wouldn't have appointed them if Church of England people of equivalent calibre were available.

> The governors would insist on Christians for permanent appointments. In an emergency it would be possible we might appoint teachers of other faiths but improbable. This would only happen, for example, if we have an LEA supply teacher on a termly contract. A non-Christian would not be appointed to a post here and this includes nominal Christians.

Two other factors were highlighted as playing an important part in decisions on staff appointments. First, the power of the local incumbent and second whether close links were maintained with the parish church. A headteacher in discussing his experience in two primary schools illustrates this point:

> In my previous school the parish was Low Church-Evangelical and we had one Hindu teacher. The vicar in this parish would not countenance appointing teachers of other faiths. The ethos in this school is high Anglo-Catholic.

In schools with teachers from different religious backgrounds on the teaching staff all but two headteachers said they made a valuable contribution to the life of the school. Furthermore, they were seen as providing a valuable link with their local religious communities.

The scarcity of a multi-faith teaching staff in church schools is matched by headteachers' comments which reveal, in general, a low commitment to religious diversity.

Having discussed current staff appointment procedures it is evident that the underlying policies adopted attempt to maintain an integrity of the trust deeds which give expression to founders' intentions. It is important to recall that a concern to educate the children of the poor was a prime factor of the church's involvement in education. The first annual report of the National Society states that church schools were established to:

> ... educate the poor in suitable learning, works of industry and the principles of the Christian religion according to the established church.[1]

Church schools are sometimes accused of 'being selective' in their pupil intake.[2] The Socialist Education Association published a discussion document which raises a number of questions for church schools. The document states that in pursuing a 'privileged intake' some church schools in urban areas are likely to have 'more high attaining pupils than the local county schools'; a 'skewed social intake' and a smaller percentage of working class children than the local county schools. It is impossible to prove or disprove conclusively whether these claims have any validity without a detailed empirical analysis of a number of factors. Information would need to be collected in a systematic way on the social backgrounds of pupils transferring to secondary schools, details of parents first choice of schools and details of pupils offered or refused a place at church secondary schools.

An attempt was made, however, to collect information on the backgrounds of pupils in a sample of London schools. Information was obtained using four measurements. First, the percentage of pupils from single-parent families; second the percentage of pupils eligible for free school meals; third, information on parents' occupation; and finally, statistics of pupils in three different academic ability groups. Statistics have been obtained for ten matching county, church secondary and primary schools. This sample is a 100 per cent sample of paired church and county schools in the Inner London Education Authority. In addition, statistics cover the remaining church secondary and primary schools in this authority which were not paired with county schools.

The following table provides details of the proportion of pupils eligible for free school meals:

Faith, Culture and the Dual System

TABLE 13:   Percentage of pupils eligible for free school meals in a sample of county and church schools

	County	Church secondary	Church primary
Area 1	45.77	33.75*	10.23*
Area 2	44.99	45.56	53.19
Area 3	37.14	27.13*	8.61*
Area 4	64.39	49.42*	36.90
Area 5	40.36	37.11*	73.67
Area 6	73.67	60.23	93.70
Area 7	38.15	44.85	75.88*
Area 8	40.03	29.46*	51.31*
Area 9	52.96	39.08*	41.92*
Area 10	41.62	36.34	47.75*

* Over-subscribed church schools

Turning to look at the comparative statistics for the percentage of pupils eligible for free school meals in county and church secondary schools, eight out of ten county schools have a higher percentage of pupils eligible for free meals than their matching church schools. In six of these county schools the percentage differences range from 10 to 16 per cent. In the remaining two county schools the percentage difference is smaller at 3 and 5 per cent respectively. In one area both the county and church have 45 per cent of pupils eligible for free school meals. In the only church school which has a higher percentage of these pupils the figure is 8 per cent higher than the paired county school. As can be seen the majority of county schools have a higher percentage of pupils receiving free school meals than their matching church schools.

These statistics show, however, that while church secondary schools do not have as high a percentage of pupils from disadvantaged homes they account for over 25 per cent of pupils in each of these schools.

The comparative statistics for church secondary and primary schools will be discussed in conjunction with the statistics in table 14. This table provides statistics on the percentage of pupils eligible for school meals in an additional eight paired church secondary and primary schools.

When the statistics in tables 13 and 14 are combined they illustrate that two-thirds of the church primary schools have a higher percentage of pupils receiving free school meals than their matching church secondary schools. In nine of these primary schools the percentage differences range from 21 per cent to 43 per cent. In the remaining four schools the difference between primary and secondary is between 3 and 11 per cent respectively.

Aspects of Diversity

TABLE 14: *Percentage of pupils eligible for free school meals in a sample of church secondary and primary schools*

	Church secondary	Church primary
Area 11	24.21*	55.34
Area 12	14.52*	50.56
Area 13	16.18*	19.28
Area 14	30.17*	14.56*
Area 15	37.34*	3.67*
Area 16	27.91*	27.27*
Area 17	24.30*	66.33
Area 18	34.84*	75.88*

* Over-subscribed church schools

TABLE 15: *Percentage of pupils from single parent families in a sample of county and church schools*

	County	Church secondary	Church primary
Area 1	29.58	32.73*	26.85*
Area 2	36.36	36.07	33.37
Area 3	27.43	15.55*	14.89*
Area 4	27.22	35.13*	16.58
Area 5	24.93	28.47*	18.35
Area 6	28.92	26.39	13.89
Area 7	22.22	32.46	68.87*
Area 8	21.83	17.65*	16.68*
Area 9	29.93	25.86*	21.42*
Area 10	25.28	21.22*	40.04*

* Over-subscribed schools

In nine of the eighteen primary schools pupils receiving free school meals account for over 50 per cent of pupils in these schools. Only one secondary school falls into this category.

The comparative statistics for matching church secondary and primary schools raise some important questions. First, to what extent do admissions policies in church secondary schools work against pupils from disadvantaged or deprived backgrounds? Second, to what extent are pupils from disadvantaged backgrounds further deprived by admission policies in popular over-subscribed secondary schools? Eight of the fifteen over-subscribed secondary schools do have a smaller percentage of pupils on free school meals than their matching primary schools.

Table 15 provides details of the distribution of pupils from single-parent families.

These statistics demonstrate that six out of ten county schools have a slightly higher percentage of pupils from single-parent families than

61

Faith, Culture and the Dual System

TABLE 16: Percentage of pupils from single parent families in a sample of church secondary and primary schools

	Church secondary	Church primary
Area 11	18.06*	68.42
Area 12	24.64*	26.61
Area 13	22.93	24.35
Area 14	26.45*	14.29*
Area 15	23.54*	3.62*
Area 16	18.49*	14.70*
Area 17	29.10	71.48
Area 18	32.59*	68.87*

* Over-subscribed schools

their matching church schools. The percentage differences, however, are relatively small ranging from less than 1 per cent to 4 per cent in five of these schools and 12 per cent in the remaining school.

When the statistics in table 15 are combined with the statistics in Table 16 it is clear that church secondary schools have a higher percentage of pupils from single-parent families than their matching primary schools. In eleven out of eighteen church secondary schools pupils from single-parent families represent a higher percentage of the pupil population than their paired primary schools.

These statistics suggest that admissions policies at secondary level do not exclude pupils from stressful home backgrounds.

The most popular measurements of social class are those used by the Registrar General.[3] The five broad categories are socio-economic in character and represent (i) professional and similar occupations, for example, doctors, lawyers; (ii) intermediate occupations, for example, retailers, teachers; (iii) skilled and clerical workers, for example, clerical staff, shop assistants; (iv) semi-skilled occupations, for example, bus conductors; (v) unskilled occupations, most kinds of labourers. While occupational groupings are used as indicators of social class this measurement is not without its problems. Wives are included in their husband's group regardless of their own occupations. In addition, family needs sometimes require single-parent mothers to take casual work of low status.

The Inner London Education Authority provided details of parental occupational groupings of pupils in the schools in the sample. These occupational groups are divided into three very broad categories — non-manual, skilled-manual and semi-unskilled. Two additional categories are included which provide statistics on the percentage of

Aspects of Diversity

TABLE 17: Cross-tabulation of parental occupations of pupils in a sample of county and church schools (percentage)

	Occupational Groups				
	Non-manual	Skilled manual	Semi-skilled	Not employed	Absent unknown
County 1	14.0	27.5	25.4	23.0	10.2
Church (S) 1	18.9	21.4	40.9	13.7	4.94
Church (P) 1	35.1	49.1	12.3	3.45	0.00
County 2	27.5	24.1	22.4	18.2	7.77
Church (S) 2	12.9	11.3	27.3	26.0	22.05
Church (P) 2	25.5	11.1	22.3	17.8	23.04
County 3	28.5	25.0	18.8	24.3	3.38
Church (S) 3	59.3	22.6	11.4	5.50	6.55
Church (P) 3	76.2	14.4	2.2	6.09	1.10
County 4	8.69	22.1	24.6	36.9	7.74
Church (S) 4	16.6	37.1	19.9	17.3	14.2
Church (P) 4	—	—	—	—	—
County 5	12.7	31.2	28.2	23.4	4.56
Church (S) 5	7.36	8.28	9.01	9.02	66.3
Church (P) 5	2.64	16.1	45.2	36.1	0.0
County 6	3.17	7.77	34.3	46.6	8.13
Church (S) 6	6.28	15.4	33.3	31.5	15.5
Church (P) 6	0.71	9.35	15.1	74.8	0.0
County 7	8.86	24.3	21.1	16.3	29.5
Church (S) 7	20.9	29.2	29.9	17.3	2.78
Church (P) 7	8.42	7.38	50.6	33.6	0.00
County 8	8.05	34.6	37.3	15.8	4.28
Church (S) 8	27.6	41.2	18.8	11.2	1.11
Church (P) 8	18.1	35.1	19.8	27.0	0.00
County 9	18.2	16.8	15.9	28.4	20.7
Church (S) 9	25.5	31.9	25.2	15.9	1.55
Church (S) 9	18.8	9.27	41.4	21.3	9.27
County 10	24.8	21.0	29.4	14.7	10.00
Church (S) 10	33.6	33.7	16.6	14.2	1.79
Church (P) 10	37.5	24.2	20.0	12.5	5.84

pupils whose parents are unemployed and a category where figures were unavailable (see tables 17 and 18).

The statistics in table 17 demonstrate that 80 per cent of church schools have a higher percentage of pupils whose parents are non-manual workers. However, in only two schools are these differences very marked — for one school it is 30 per cent and in the other it is 20 per cent. Both these church schools are popular over-subscribed schools drawing on wide catchment areas. It is easy to envisage that on a local level these schools would be associated with 'a skewed social' intake.

Combining the figures in tables 17 and 18 it is apparent two-thirds

Faith, Culture and the Dual System

TABLE 18: Cross-tabulation of parental occupations of pupils in a sample of church secondary and primary schools (percentage)

Church Schools Areas	Non-manual	Skilled manual	Semi-skilled	Not employed	Absent unknown
Secondary 11*	37.2	23.5	8.03	1.78	29.5
Primary 11	11.8	13.7	25.5	49.0	0.0
Secondary 13*	61.3	24.3	6.70	5.71	1.97
Primary 13	46.0	21.2	27.9	4.87	0.00
Secondary 15*	27.0	26.4	18.9	16.3	11.3
Primary 15*	86.7	9.99	2.20	1.10	0.0
Secondary 16*	26.0	33.3	27.2	0.90	12.6
Primary 16*	21.8	36.4	16.3	21.8	3.61
Secondary 17*	38.6	41.0	9.80	10.4	0.27
Primary 17*	12.8	3.60	51.1	32.6	0.00
Secondary 18*	13.7	16.8	36.0	13.3	20.3
Primary 18*	8.42	7.38	50.6	33.6	0.0

Note: Statistics were not provided for schools in areas 12 and 14

of church secondary schools have a higher percentage of pupils whose parents are in non-manual occupations. In two of the matching schools the difference is as high as 26 per cent.

There is also a far higher incidence of parental unemployment among pupils in county schools. The statistics in Table 17 show that seven out of ten county schools have a higher percentage of pupils who have at least one parent unemployed when compared with their matching church schools.

In chapter 2 reference is made to the practice of banding in the Inner London Education Authority where each year pupils due to transfer to secondary schools are placed in three bands. Schools are required to accept pupils in accordance with a 'balance of ability' formula drawn up by the Authority each year. This banding arrangement provides an important measurement for the composition of pupils in county and church schools. In an attempt to ascertain whether church schools had a higher percentage of high attaining pupils statistics were obtained for ten matching church and county schools.

Table 19 provides details on whether secondary schools have a full quota of pupils in the three ability groups — Band 1 pupils of above average ability; Band 2 pupils of average ability; and Band 3 pupils of below average ability.

Turning to look at pupil quotas in Band 1 table 19 shows that four matching church and county schools have their full quota of pupils in the

Aspects of Diversity

TABLE 19: Quota of pupils in bands 1, 2, 3 in church and county schools

	Band 1 Full Quota	Band 2 Full Quota	Band 3 Full Quota
County 1	No	Yes	Yes
Church 1	Yes	Yes	Yes
County 2	No	Yes	Yes
Church 2	No	Yes	Yes
County 3	No	No	No
Church 3	Yes	Yes	No
County 4	Yes	Yes	Yes
Church 4	Yes	Yes	No
County 5	Yes	Yes	Yes
Church 5	Yes	Yes	Yes
County 6	No	No	No
Church 6	No	Yes	No
County 7	Yes	Yes	Yes
Church 7	No	No	Yes
County 8	No	No	Yes
Church 8	Yes	Yes	No
County 9	No	No	Yes
Church 9	Yes	Yes	Yes
County 10	No	No	Yes
Church 10	Yes	Yes	Yes

Note: Statistics relate to September 1983

above average ability groups (Band 1). Five church schools have their full quota of pupils in Band 1 while their matching county schools have not filled all the available places. Only one county school has a full quota of Band 1 pupils while the matching church school is under-subscribed in this band. In other words, 50 per cent of church schools have a higher percentage of pupils with above average ability than their paired county scho'

A simil schools have again, five c the number matching co Band 2 whil

Ten cou pupils. Two church schools failed to fill all the available places in this band.

ERRATUM

Page 64   line 22 for 'four' read 'two'.

Page 65   line 14 for 'Ten' read 'Eight'; for 'eight' read 'six'.
          line 15 for 'Two' read 'Four'.
          line 17 for '90' read '70'.

Page 66   line 1 for '50' read '30'.

The overall picture that emerges is that 90 per cent of church schools succeed in getting their full quota of pupils who are above

65

average ability whereas for county schools the comparable figure is 50 per cent.

Not only do these statistics provide evidence to support the view expressed in the Socialist Education Association's discussion document that admissions policies in church schools result in a 'skewed attainment intake (with more high attaining pupils than are taken into local county comprehensives)' but they also raise an important question. To what extent does the practice of drawing pupils from very wide catchment areas contribute to the high level of above average ability pupils found in church schools?

One factor that may go some way to explaining the reasons why church schools manage to attract high attaining pupils concerns their previous status. Six of the ten church secondary schools had a grammar school status prior to reorganization along comprehensive lines while only two matching county schools previously had a grammar school status. The remaining matching schools previously had a secondary modern status or they derive from an amalgamation of grammar and secondary modern schools. If church schools today continue to be regarded locally by parents as the 'grammar school' and if schools continue to retain the right to interview prospective pupils, the view of parents and the admission practice of the school will combine to create an imbalance within the local education provision.

As Dave Picton points out:—

> In a situation of falling rolls, when such schools have a reputation locally as grammar schools and parental choice is the predominant factor in allocating pupils, this can quickly lead to a two-tier system.[4]

This is particularly true when the church school is seen by parents as a 'franking machine'[5] to stamp the words 'certified success' on most of its pupils at the expense of the deprived and the disadvantaged.

In the previous chapter we saw that just over half (51 per cent) of the parents in the study associated church schools with academic reputation and good discipline. Where church schools are more popular than county schools they may be as the Runnymede Trust points out, 'wittingly or unwittingly propping up racism and racial disadvantage.'[6] This is particularly relevant in areas where church school admissions policies have an adverse effect on children of non-Christian faiths. As we have seen policies can, and do exclude or discriminate against, pupils from non-Christian ethnic minority groups.

A crucial question concerns whether church schools are a service provided by the church. For, as the Runnymede Trust has pointed out,

Aspects of Diversity

TABLE 19: *Quota of pupils in bands 1, 2, 3 in church and county schools*

	Band 1 Full Quota	Band 2 Full Quota	Band 3 Full Quota
County 1	No	Yes	Yes
Church 1	Yes	Yes	Yes
County 2	No	Yes	Yes
Church 2	No	Yes	Yes
County 3	No	No	No
Church 3	Yes	Yes	No
County 4	Yes	Yes	Yes
Church 4	Yes	Yes	No
County 5	Yes	Yes	Yes
Church 5	Yes	Yes	Yes
County 6	No	No	No
Church 6	No	Yes	No
County 7	Yes	Yes	Yes
Church 7	No	No	Yes
County 8	No	No	Yes
Church 8	Yes	Yes	No
County 9	No	No	Yes
Church 9	Yes	Yes	Yes
County 10	No	No	Yes
Church 10	Yes	Yes	Yes

Note: Statistics relate to September 1983

above average ability groups (Band 1). Five church schools have their full quota of pupils in Band 1 while their matching county schools have not filled all the available places. Only one county school has a full quota of Band 1 pupils while the matching church school is under-subscribed in this band. In other words, 50 per cent of church schools have a higher percentage of pupils with above average ability than their paired county schools.

A similar pattern emerges for Band 2. Four church and county schools have a full quota of pupils who are of average ability. Once again, five church schools have a full quota of pupils in this band while the number of pupils in this group falls short of the quota in the matching county schools. Only one church school is under-subscribed in Band 2 while its matching county school is over-subscribed.

Ten county and eight church schools have their full quota of Band 3 pupils. Two church schools failed to fill all the available places in this band.

The overall picture that emerges is that 90 per cent of church schools succeed in getting their full quota of pupils who are above

65

average ability whereas for county schools the comparable figure is 50 per cent.

Not only do these statistics provide evidence to support the view expressed in the Socialist Education Association's discussion document that admissions policies in church schools result in a 'skewed attainment intake (with more high attaining pupils than are taken into local county comprehensives)' but they also raise an important question. To what extent does the practice of drawing pupils from very wide catchment areas contribute to the high level of above average ability pupils found in church schools?

One factor that may go some way to explaining the reasons why church schools manage to attract high attaining pupils concerns their previous status. Six of the ten church secondary schools had a grammar school status prior to reorganization along comprehensive lines while only two matching county schools previously had a grammar school status. The remaining matching schools previously had a secondary modern status or they derive from an amalgamation of grammar and secondary modern schools. If church schools today continue to be regarded locally by parents as the 'grammar school' and if schools continue to retain the right to interview prospective pupils, the view of parents and the admission practice of the school will combine to create an imbalance within the local education provision.

As Dave Picton points out:—

> In a situation of falling rolls, when such schools have a reputation locally as grammar schools and parental choice is the predominant factor in allocating pupils, this can quickly lead to a two-tier system.[4]

This is particularly true when the church school is seen by parents as a 'franking machine'[5] to stamp the words 'certified success' on most of its pupils at the expense of the deprived and the disadvantaged.

In the previous chapter we saw that just over half (51 per cent) of the parents in the study associated church schools with academic reputation and good discipline. Where church schools are more popular than county schools they may be as the Runnymede Trust points out, 'wittingly or unwittingly propping up racism and racial disadvantage.'[6] This is particularly relevant in areas where church school admissions policies have an adverse effect on children of non-Christian faiths. As we have seen policies can, and do exclude or discriminate against, pupils from non-Christian ethnic minority groups.

A crucial question concerns whether church schools are a service provided by the church. For, as the Runnymede Trust has pointed out,

Aspects of Diversity

if the modern church school is a service provided by, rather than for, the church, less importance will be placed on the religious affiliations of pupils. A school working on this assumption, the Trust remarks, could decide to accept some Sikh or Muslim pupils even if there were Christians wanting to attend. The justification would be that to admit Asian pupils would be a more important service to the local community in a racist society than to admit white ones.[7] It could be considered that such an approach would continue to fulfil the intentions of the founders of the National Society in providing education for the poor and underprivileged, while continuing to provide for the needs of the worshipping community.

It is important to emphasise that when drawing upon the Runnymede Trust the disadvantaged are not equated with non-Christian minority groups only. Clearly, disadvantage whether of poverty or deprivation, cuts across racial and religious boundaries. There is a danger that in focussing on the concept of racism (although understandable in terms of their major concerns) the Runnymede Trust over simplify the reality of a situation which encompasses broader issues.

To conclude, measurements of disadvantage relating to single parent families, free school meals, parental occupation/unemployment demonstrate that county schools have a higher percentage of pupils receiving free school meals; a higher percentage of pupils from single parent families (although the percentage differences are small); a smaller percentage of pupils with parents in non-manual occupations and a higher incidence of parental unemployment than their matching church secondary schools. Finally, county schools in the sample have fewer high attaining pupils.

However, it was not possible to correlate the evidence of imbalance of disadvantaged pupils and church schools admission policies and practices. Further research is needed to identify whether, in the first instance, pupils from the different groups just mentioned applied for places in church schools and secondly, whether they expressed a preference which was not met, denying them access. The lack of empirical evidence surrounding pupil transfer from primary to secondary schools demands that opportunity is not confused with outcome.

Finally, while there is an emphasis on the church school as a religious community there is very little evidence to show that those responsible for staff appointments perceive their schools as environments where Christian teachers can learn from teachers of other faiths and at the same time bear witness to their own faith. There is a general absence of a commitment to religious diversity among the teaching staff.

Faith, Culture and the Dual System

It is certainly not reflected in practices, policies and attitudes of governing bodies. In many ways these schools are explicitly saying that they can find no common ground to share with members of other faiths that which has been entrusted to them.

Notes

1. *National Society Annual Report.* (1812/1813) p. 7.
2. Socialist Education Association. *The Dual System of Voluntary and County Schools*, p. 8.
3. These five broad categories 1–5 are used by the Registrar General in the Government's Decennial Census of Population.
4. Picton Dave. Socialist Teacher 13.
5. PAUL HARRISON used this expression in discussing educational failure in HARRISON, P. (1983) 'Life under the cutting edge' in *Inside the Inner City* London, Penguin Books, p. 285.
6. DUMMET, A. and McNEAL, J. (1981) *Race and Church Schools*, The Runnymede Trust, p. 17.
7. *Ibid.*, p. 18.

Chapter 5

School Worship and Assemblies

This chapter is concerned primarily with aims, content and provision of school worship and assembly in church and county schools. Within an empirical framework it attempts to clarify some of the issues regarding the place of worship and assembly in the life of the school. It discusses headteachers' views as to whether the idea envisaged in the 1944 Act is considered desirable or practical. In doing so, this chapter describes the two distinct approaches adopted by church and county schools in their responses to the plurality of faiths and cultures in schools. The 1944 Education Act requires that:

> ... the school day ... shall begin with collective worship on the part of all pupils in attendance at the school, and the arrangements made therefore shall provide for a single act of worship attended by all such pupils unless in the opinion of the local education authority ... the school premises are such as to make it impracticable to assemble them for that purpose.[1]

The Act also states that:

> ... the collective worship ... shall not, in any county school be distinctive of any particular religious denomination.[2]

In 1944 the Act was concerned with providing a legal basis for what was then the norm in most schools. Forty years later, a great deal of current writing on the subject of school worship calls for a reinterpretation of the Act.[3] When this Act was passed, it was commonly held that school worship should be Christian although nowhere in the Act is this specified.

Despite pressure for change, the Conservative government continues to stress the importance of school worship in the life of the school. The Swann Report in its main conclusions and recommendations states that:

Faith, Culture and the Dual System

Given the multiplicity of beliefs now present in society, it is not surprising that we have received much evidence about the difficulties generated by the requirement in the 1944 Act for a daily act of collective worship and the provision of a particular form of religious education. We therefore believe that the government, in consultation with religious and educational bodies, should look afresh at the relevant provisions of the Act to see whether alterations are called for after an interval of forty years.[4]

In reply to this recommendation Sir Keith Joseph, Secretary of State for Education and Science, declared in the House of Commons that 'We do not intend to change the present statutory requirements for collective worship and religious education in maintained schools'.

Headteachers were asked to provide details on assemblies. Table 20 provides statistics on how often assembly occurs for each pupil.

TABLE 20: *Cross-tabulation on the frequency of assembly for pupils in county and church schools*

	Daily	Four times a week	Three times a week	Twice a week	Once a week
County	3 (10.7)	3 (10.7)	5 (17.8)	10 (35.7)	7 (25.0)
Church Secondary	18 (47.3)	9 (23.6)	7 (18.4)*	4 (10.5)	–
Church Primary	22 (59.4)	11 (29.7)	4 (10.8)	–	–

*In one school, assemblies are held three times a week for forms 1, 2, 3 and four times a week for forms 4 and 5. These statistics refer to how frequently assemblies occur for each pupil including whole school assemblies, year, form or house assemblies. In the case of primary schools, form assemblies are included.

The above table shows that just under 11 per cent of county schools' pupils attend daily assemblies. Assemblies are far less frequent for pupils in county schools than is the case in church schools. In 60 per cent of county schools pupils attend assemblies no more than twice a week. In 59 per cent of church primary schools pupils attend assemblies daily. In just under half the church secondary schools (47 per cent) pupils attend a daily assembly. Only a minority of secondary schools arranged assemblies for the whole school as table 21 shows.

The statistics show that church schools hold assemblies for the whole school more frequently than county schools. The major reason given for not providing the opportunity for all pupils to assemble concerns school size. In thirteen out of nineteen county schools and in fourteen out of sixteen church secondary schools, they are either on

School Worship and Assemblies

TABLE 21: Frequency of assemblies for the whole school

	County	Church secondary
Daily	–	3
Four times a week	1	4
Three times a week	1	5
Twice a week	–	4
Once a week	7	3
Fortnightly	–	1
Twice a term	–	2
Never	19	16
Total	28	38

TABLE 22: Cross-tabulation of headteachers' classification of assemblies

	Devotional	Religious	Non-Religious	Platform for moral/social issues	Religious moral	Lower school religious upper school moral issues	Difficult to say
County	4	2	11	5	1	2	3
Church secondary	32	6	–	–	–	–	–
Church primary	35	2	–	–	–	–	–

split-level sites or the schools are too small for whole school assemblies.

Headteachers were asked how they would classify their assemblies. Their replies which fall into seven broad categories are given in table 22.

This classification was, in many cases, a difficult task for county headteachers as there is far more variation to be found in county school assemblies. Headteachers in county schools point out that different teachers take it in turn to be responsible, frequently choosing their own topic or theme. The varied backgrounds of headteachers and staff have a direct bearing on the nature of assembly as one headteacher shows. 'There is no reference to God. I personally would not feel genuine, not being a practising anything and my insincerity would destroy any effect I might like to have'. At times there is disagreement between the headteacher and staff. The resulting tension is demonstrated in the following abstract:

> In the third, fourth and fifth years there is no religious content. Assemblies are given up to football results, etc. At the moment year heads take these assemblies and they feel that children should not be exposed to religion in these assemblies but I feel they should be given the chance to make up their minds. I take the second year and there is always a religious element.

Faith, Culture and the Dual System

The general picture that emerges in county schools is the difficulty of ensuring a continuity and structure of assemblies.

The 'non-religious' category (table 22) is also used for headteachers who tended to say what they were not, rather than what they were. However, the majority in this group did specify that they were either secular or humanist. The following statements from recorded interviews illustrate this point:

> There is no scripture and no prayers. Talking more positively, assembly is multi-cultural and it is rational. There is no over-arching religious element except like harvest festival today. Today was the first time pupils have sung hymns since the carol service.

Another teacher making the same point said:

> Assemblies are basically non-religious. There is no deliberate act of worship. They are occasionally used for pupils' performances of music and drama. I doubt if we are working in the spirit of the 1944 Act. We never have a hymn or a prayer.

Headteachers were asked to provide details on the content of assembly. Their replies were then analyzed to ascertain the Christian element, the use of prayers and hymns and whether faiths other than Christianity find a place in assemblies. Details of headteachers' replies regarding the Christian content of assemblies are provided in the following table.

TABLE 23: Cross-tabulation of the christian content in school assemblies

	Always Christian	Majority have a Christian element	Often a Christian element	Rarely a Christian element	No Christian element
County	6 (21.4)	3 (10.7)	7 (25.0)	1 (3.5)	11 (39.2)
Church secondary	36 (94.7)	1 (2.6)	1 (2.6)	–	–
Church primary	35 (94.5)	1 (2.7)	1 (2.7)	–	–

At this point one major observation can be made. The Christian element in assembly finds a regular place in only a minority of county schools. The reverse is true for both primary and secondary church schools. In all but four schools assemblies are Christian in content.

Fourteen county schools (50 per cent) never use prayers during assembly. Even fewer county schools sing hymns. Singing of hymns occurs in only eight county schools (28 per cent). In two of these schools the singing of hymns only occurs among the younger pupils.

School Worship and Assemblies

Turning to look at assemblies in church secondary schools prayer takes place in thirty-six schools (95 per cent). The singing of hymns is less popular and occurs in twenty-five schools (66 per cent). A similar picture emerges for church primary schools. Only one school does not include prayers and hymns are sung in twenty-four schools (64 per cent).

A cross-tabulation on the content of assembly and the geographical location of schools produced some interesting findings. In ten (52 per cent of the Greater London sample) out of the nineteen county schools in London there is no Christian content to their assemblies. The inclusion of prayers occurs in seven (37 per cent) out of nineteen London county schools. The singing of hymns occurs in two schools (10 per cent) and in one it is restricted to the lower forms.

For schools in the north-west Region and the West Midlands the picture for county schools is very different. There is only one school where assemblies rarely have a Christian content. In five schools there is always a Christian element and in the remaining three schools the majority of assemblies have a Christian content. In other words, in 88 per cent of the schools visited outside London the majority of assemblies have a Christian content. In eight out of nine schools, prayer features in assemblies and the singing of hymns occurs in seven out of nine county schools.

Seventeen county headteachers provided statistics on the religious affiliation of pupils. A cross-tabulation on the religious affiliation of pupils and the content of school assemblies shows that the greater the diversity of beliefs among pupils and the higher the proportion of pupils claiming no religious allegiance the more infrequently assemblies with Christian content occur in London schools.

The same holds true for only one school outside the London area. In this school Christian pupils are in the minority and Muslim, Sikh and Hindu children account for 65 per cent of all pupils. However, four schools continue to include prayers or hymns in assembly despite the fact that non-Christian faiths account for 9, 22, 27 and 83 per cent of the pupil population in these schools.

One headteacher in the West Midlands illustrates how he tries to provide assemblies which cater for the different needs of pupils:

> The main aim is to provide a corporate spirit. In this school we cannot run a traditional Christian assembly. There is a separate Muslim assembly once a week. A major aim is to allay their fears (Muslim children) that their own culture will not be ignored and also to allay the fears of the indigenous children that their

Faith, Culture and the Dual System

culture will not be swamped. Sometimes the content is Christian, sometimes we invite people from different religions. We try to be fair to the religious backgrounds of all pupils.

The statistics on the religious affiliation of pupils in London schools show that in seven out of thirteen schools pupils belonging to atheist and agnostic backgrounds (included in these statistics are pupils whose religious affiliation is unknown by headteacher) accounted for over 35 per cent of all pupils and in a further two schools the percentage is over 50 per cent. In seven of these schools pupils belonging to non-Christian faiths represent a smaller percentage than pupils from atheist and agnostic backgrounds.

Only one headteacher outside London recorded the presence of pupils who are either atheist or agnostic.

One explanation for the geographical variations and the content of school assemblies is that the presence of children from agnostic and atheistic backgrounds is more likely to influence decisions regarding the content of assembly in making them more secular. The statistics provided raise the question as to how far the presence of children of non-Christian faiths in the school population has any major impact on the content of assembly.

Church schools both primary and secondary continue to hold assemblies that are mostly Christian (there are a few exceptions) and the percentage of pupils belonging to faiths other than Christianity does not affect the content to any great extent.

Headteachers were asked what they considered to be the main aims of assembly. Their replies fell into three main categories — religious, social and educational.[5] The religious category includes replies such as 'coming together to offer service to God, corporate prayers, corporate worship, to link everyday life with the spiritual and to impart Christian values'. (There is, however, an educational aim here). Replies that have been grouped under the social category are in the majority of cases linked to the school environment. They include 'to bring disparate parts of the school together, to provide a calm start to the day, to be seen as a corporate body, to bring us together as a school community of shared values and a means of communicating to human form'.

The third category 'educational' includes replies — 'to develop understanding', 'to raise moral, social and ethical questions', 'a time for reflection', 'to stimulate moral awareness' and 'to provide a link with the curriculum'. The following table shows the aims mentioned.

Only a minority of county headteachers mentioned religious aims.

TABLE 24: Cross-tabulation on aims of assemblies in county and church schools

	Religious	Social	Education
County	6	13	14
Church secondary	35	13	16
Church primary	36	4	30

Note: Sixty-four teachers mentioned more than one aim. If two or more aims belonging to the same category were mentioned they counted as one.

Assemblies are frequently valued for reasons other than religious ones; they are used to heighten awareness of ethical, moral and social issues including current affairs. Assemblies are seen as having an educational potential and providing a link with the curriculum especially in the areas of social and moral education. They also play an important role in reinforcing the ethos of the school and establishing a community spirit.

County headteachers in the majority of schools stressed that pupils do not assemble for collective worship as traditionally understood. Indeed, our research shows that only a minority of county schools regularly have assemblies that have a religious content. In response to the question — do you think that assemblies in your school should be an introduction to Christian worship? — 24 county headteachers (86 per cent) affirmed that assemblies should not be an introduction to Christian worship. Three headteachers (11 per cent) valued the Christian link. One headteacher (3 per cent) was not sure.

The main reasons given for not including Christian worship in county school assemblies concerned the religious and cultural diversity of the pupils. The following quotations represent the majority view:

> No, because I am conscious of the fact of the many different cultures. If parents want that they can go to ... Church of England school.

> No, a significant number of the children are not Christian and it would make them feel faulty in some way.

> No, I don't think it would be appropriate for the population we are dealing with. I am thinking particularly about the other faiths within the school. In a school of such varied faiths it is not possible. You cannot expect children of other faiths to participate in worship.

For one headteacher a distinction is drawn between Christian morality and Christian worship:

Faith, Culture and the Dual System

> Given the mixture we have in the school I can't see it makes sense for the whole of the community. Christian morality has a place in the school but not Christian worship. The two are quite separate. Also I am not committed myself and probably agnostic, the kids would see through me if I try to emphasise worship.

While two headteachers saw assemblies as providing pupils with an introduction to worship, they were both opposed to Christian worship. Using a broad definition of worship one teacher comments — 'Assembly is the place for introducing worship but not Christian worship. If I can inspire awe and wonder in any assembly then I am introducing worship'. The other headteacher distinguishes between participating in and the understanding of an act of worship — 'No, I don't see it as the school's job to get children to participate in acts of worship but it is necessary for them to understand acts of worship'.

A clear picture emerges from our discussions with county headteachers regarding school worship. In the majority of county schools collective worship is seen as an inappropriate activity because both pupils and staff encompass a wide range of religious beliefs and secular views. Collective worship is not seen as reflecting the life and ethos of the whole school community. It is for these reasons that headteachers recognize the inappropriateness of compulsory collective worship laid down by the 1944 Act and instead stress the importance of assemblies which promote a sense of community, emphasise values such as respect for others, tolerance, justice, compassion and responsibility, and allow for the affirmation of values that are significant within the whole school community. These teachers take as their starting point, the diversity of pupils', and teachers' backgrounds.

The three county headteachers who said Christian worship is appropriate in their schools, take as their starting point the Christian children in the school — 'In any year a number of children will be regular church-goers. School worship enables these pupils to experience the experiential dimension to religion within the school environment'.

For the majority of church schools (both primary and secondary) school worship is seen as a collective act of worship and central feature in the life of the school. What is clear is that worship is Christian and in line with Church of England practice. The majority of schools teach distinctive beliefs and practices and they are frequently involved in liturgical activity as a worshipping community. In most schools, assembly and Christian worship are synonymous. In addition, there

School Worship and Assemblies

tends to be a continuity of structure — 'We follow the order of the Christian year', 'Assembly is distinctively Anglican'. Another headteacher describes assembly in his school in the following way:

> Assembly is the central feature of the daily life. It is the first thing that happens and all the children attend. The assembly is the central part of the teaching about the churches and the Christian background which the church supports. We have an evening assembly as well as a morning one. We do not use modern philosophers saying we ought to be good. Assembly follows a stable regular pattern. There is an introductory Collect which relates to the Saint's day. We do according to the church's calendar. Then there will be canticles and responses by the choir. The third aspect is a reading ... Then there will be prayers, a hymn, a blessing and organ music as the procession goes out. It is like a small formal Anglican service.

Although there was a small percentage of children who were not Christians, their parents were asked not to withdraw them from assembly.

Collective worship is seen as contributing to the educational development of all pupils. It provides the opportunity to see Christians involved in worship and it is 'concerned with spiritual growth'. All but two secondary headteachers confirm the ideal that Christian worship is of central importance in the life of their schools. Six headteachers, while stressing the ideal, had doubts whether pupils would agree. There is often a gap between the ideal and what happens in reality as one headteacher observes — 'It should be but it is not. Sacramental life definitely is not. Worship should be but it isn't. We asked the children what they think about assemblies and we realize that it is not central in their school lives. Some of them don't even understand what they are doing there'.

In church primary schools, and to a lesser extent in church secondary schools assemblies provide an important link with religious education classes. They are often a leader lesson for areas of study. Stories concerning the life of Jesus are linked to values such as caring, compassion and respect.

Headteachers in church secondary schools were asked whether Christian worship is inappropriate if the common commitment it assumes does not exist. Thirty headteachers (79 per cent) said it is appropriate. Three (8 per cent) said, yes it might be, but were not too sure. Another four (10 per cent) thought it inappropriate and one headteacher preferred not to answer the question. Replies affirming the appropriateness of school worship can be grouped into three main categories — educational, school ethos and mission. The educational reason is illustrated in the following way — 'My educational philosophy is that no school experience should be withheld from young people. They should be open to as many experiences as possible and the Christian experience is one of them. Christianity is the religion of our country and all children regardless of their backgrounds should be made aware of its significance.' For others, school worship 'facilitates understanding'. It provides the opportunity 'to understand what worship means to the religiously committed'. In addition, 'school worship attempts to communicate the Christian faith, and it makes explicit what is implicit in the classroom'. School worship for non-Christians is seen as enabling them to understand Christian worship in an informed way through religious language, concepts and symbols.

Christian worship is seen as playing a major part in contributing to the ethos of the school. As a concept, ethos is indeed complex and notoriously difficult to define. Rutter talks of ethos as 'the values, attitudes and behaviours which are characteristic of the school as a whole'.[6] Dancy, using the Shorter Oxford Dictionary's definition of ethos as 'the prevalent tone or sentiment of a people or community', observes that the word 'prevalent' implies that 'the tone is more powerful than other competing 'tones' and will go on being so —'. In addition he points out that the word 'prevalent' 'holds sway in the sense of being shared by *either* most members of the community *or* the most powerful or influential *or* some weighted mixture of the two'.[7]

Headteachers linked Christian worship and ethos particularly with their school's Christian Foundation, beliefs, values and attitudes and in providing an environment in which Christian principles are applied and percolate into all school activities and relationships.

For some, the concepts of 'mission' and 'maintenance' find an important place in collective school worship. As one headteacher said: 'The Christian Church from the time of St. Paul has preached its message to all. This is what we are in the business for and to do other would neither serve God nor man. Other faiths respect us for the sincerity and tenacity with which we hold our faith'. Another headteacher in confirming the appropriateness of school worship, poses the question — 'Is Christian mission in a non-Christian country inappropriate?'. The frequency of the word 'mission' in church schools points to a need to examine the theological assumptions that lie behind the

School Worship and Assemblies

concept of mission in church schools and its educational implications. Kevin Nichols, in discussing mission states:

> 'Mission' seems ordinarily to mean the bringing to others some valued state of affairs. We ought to look more closely at the two elements in this definition. The first is the act of bringing to others. It involves the activities of spreading and propagating, of changing and converting others. It entails that the valued state of affairs is not regarded as a personal possession to be hoarded, but as something which ought to be communicated as widely as possible.[8]

New questions arise for church schools where there are different faiths represented in the school population. There is the need to question and reflect on what is the contemporary understanding of 'mission' and how far the concept of mission is compatible with educational principles and whether there is an intolerable mismatch between the two.

In the majority of county and church schools the religious diversity of pupils is not given expression in school assemblies. Six county schools (21 per cent) hold assemblies which involve looking at different cultural and religious groups. In these schools 'assemblies might be connected with the Bible, the Koran or about a Hindu or Buddhist teacher'; other assemblies 'are sometimes linked with a story about China or the life of Gandhi; how Greeks celebrate Easter; or the performance of Asian dances'.

Six primary headteachers (16 per cent) in church schools said the content of assembly includes looking at other faiths. Sometimes they included Passover, Festival of Lights, depending on the calendar, or a Jewish or Hindu story, particularly when BBC broadcasts were used.

In seven church secondary schools (18 per cent) faiths other than Christianity were given expression in assembly. In one of these schools a Muslim assembly is held once a week. The Immam comes to the school to take this assembly which contains instruction as well.

In primary schools the majority of headteachers are confident about the approach adopted to school worship in a multifaith situation. However, a number of teachers expressed anxiety and questioned what is the correct approach in a multifaith situation. The gap between headteachers' views is extreme as their replies to the question — 'How are different cultures and faiths expressed within your school?' show:

> They are not overtly expressed but they are respected and not

Faith, Culture and the Dual System

minimized or dismissed. In a C of E school they should not be expressed.

Another headteacher distinguishes between multifaith and multicultural education.

> We discourage multifaith education but allow for multicultural education within a Christian context ... When children come to this school we put them into four teams. Two of the teams are named after members of ethnic minorities — an Indian Christian and a West Indian Christian. Children do projects on other cultures too.

Another primary headteacher also distinguishes between culture and faith.

> It is necessary to distinguish between faiths and cultures. Different cultures are expressed. We have a definite policy of encouraging children to find out and encouraging them to acquire an understanding of different cultures.

A headteacher of a church school with a very high percentage of Muslim and Hindu pupils said 'We are floundering. We find ourselves in a new situation and do not know how to react. In the meantime the school continues to hold collective worship with all pupils participating'. The word 'participating' implies that children are not just observing worship but they are taking an active part and it raises important questions concerning the aims and objectives of school worship in a multifaith context.

How to present different faiths is a stumbling block for some primary headteachers particularly in inner London schools. Sometimes it is a result of lack of knowledge or uncertainty as to how the church school should respond as the following shows:

> We have books in the library on other faiths but I am not sure if it is the role of the church school to do this. Also, I know so little about what Muslims and Sikhs do and believe that it would be an impertinence for me to try to teach them about their own faiths.

The following highlights other difficulties:

> One of the great dilemmas I faced here when I came was that we have a Christian assembly and I am faced with about 40 per cent of brown faces who are perhaps betraying their own religion when we take them through the Christian practices, for example,

School Worship and Assemblies

we say Jesus Christ is the Son of God and this is against the Muslim view of Jesus Christ as prophet.

There was evidence to show that in church secondary schools there is little recognition given to the diversity which exists within Christianity. Many West Indian children have their own distinctive expression of Christianity and place a different emphasis on the ritual dimension. Teachers sometimes found it difficult to respond positively to the diversity within Christianity as one headteacher demonstrates:

> We have a large number of Caribbean Pentecostal children, they do not recognize what we teach as correct. As far as I see their form of Christianity is an extreme Victorian attitude to religion mixed with a Pentecostal way of worship. They will not take part in assemblies although it is a Christian school, it is based on Anglicanism and they are expected to take part but they are disruptive.

The statutory right of parents to withdraw their children from school worship is rarely used in church primary and secondary schools. In thirty-five (92 per cent) secondary and thirty-three (84 per cent) primary schools no pupil withdrew from assembly. All pupils in these schools are expected to join in collective worship regardless of their own faith. The general view expressed is that in sending a child to a church school, parents agree (some by signing a form) to allow their child to participate in the full life of the school. There is no provision for what is often seen as 'opting out' as the following comments show:

> All participate. If you come to the school you accept it is a Christian school and you expect to play a full part in the worship of the school. Everyone goes to church and there are no objections even from those of other faiths.

Another teacher making the same point said:

> No withdrawals. Acceptance at the school is acceptance of assemblies and Christian ethic. There is tacit acceptance of a Christian ethos. Also, to withdraw a child from RE or assembly would be pointless because the Christian ethic permeates the whole life of the school.

In sixteen county schools there is a small percentage of pupils who withdraw from assembly. The Jehovah's Witnesses are in the most likely group to consistently withdraw. Only small numbers of Muslim pupils withdraw.

Faith, Culture and the Dual System

Pupils from just over a quarter of county schools visit the local church to hold a school service. This is usually the carol service. In addition, just under half the county schools visit the local churches as part of a religious education programme. In one school pupils participate in special music services at different churches.

The church primary school is viewed by headteachers as an extension of the church and the activities in schools continue without change of emphasis to reflect this link. Twenty-one (56 per cent) primary headteachers see their schools as an extension of the parish church. Another seven headteachers (18 per cent) who do not see their schools as an extension of the parish church nevertheless stressed that close links were maintained. The local incumbent is a frequent visitor and he is seen as having an important pastoral role in primary schools. In thirty-three primary schools he visits pupils in their classroom and he frequently leads assembly. Only two headteachers are dissatisfied with their local incumbent and in both cases it is due to a lack of involvement and interest. One of these headteachers when asked about the partnership between the local incumbent and the school described the partnership as 'pitiful'. There are no regular visits to the school and no regular church services. In thirty-three primary schools all pupils regularly attend church service in the local church.

All headteachers in church secondary schools confirmed that their church school is an active Christian community linked to the church of which it is part. Visits to the local church find a regular place in the life of the school. Holy Communion services are held regularly and the clergy frequently lead assembly. Table 25 provides statistics for all three activities in schools.

TABLE 25: *Frequencies for church-related activities in church secondary schools*

	Number of Schools		
	Holy Communion	Church Service	Assemblies led by clergy
At least once a week	8	1	11
Monthly	8	2	1
1–3 times a term	9	11	8
4–8 times a term	4	–	15
Special days	5	19	–
Never	4	5*	3
Total	38	38	38

* Three of these schools have their own chapel where services are held. Another fourteen schools have their own chapel but continue to have some school services in the local church.

School Worship and Assemblies

In twenty-one (55 per cent) secondary schools attendance at church services is compulsory for all pupils, despite the fact that attendance cannot be compulsory under section 25 of the 1944 Act which allows the right of withdrawal. We have seen that in many schools an acceptance of a school place involves an acceptance of participating in the full life of the school. The majority of schools do not insist on compulsory attendance at Communion services — although thirteen schools (34 per cent) continue to do so. In two of these schools attendance at the Communion service is compulsory for forms 1 to 3, for the older pupils attendance is voluntary. In another school where 40 per cent of the pupils are Muslims, Hindus and Sikhs, attendance is compulsory for Christian pupils.

In fifteen schools where church attendance is compulsory the pupil population consists of pupils from a variety of religious backgrounds. In nine of these schools children from non-Christian faiths represent up to 1 per cent of pupils. In the remaining schools the percentage of pupils belonging to faiths other than Christianity represents 9, 15, 20, 40 and 43 per cent of pupils in each school. Four of these schools also require compulsory attendance at Holy Communion services. In two schools children of non-Christian faiths represented under 2 per cent of pupils, in the remaining two schools they accounted for 20 per cent of all pupils in one school and 40 per cent in the other.

When the question was put to headteachers in church schools — what do children of faiths other than Christianity do during assembly and school worship-the majority of headteachers said all participate. Again we come up against the activity of participating. For some, this involved joining in the responses, bodily movements such as kneeling or bowing one's head. For others participating means simply attending and observing.

In church schools where all the pupils are Christians, Christian worship, sacramental life and participation in the Church services fit the Durham Report's definition 'Christian worship ... refers to offering in corporate gatherings of prayer and praise to God through Christ'.[9] The use of the word 'corporate' suggests a community of faith and a unity of intention. The expressive aspect of worship 'which concerns the intentional response of the worshipper to God' is appropriate in a community of believers where there is a recognition and confirmation of shared values and beliefs. Worship in church schools articulates a system of meaning and prevents it being lost from sight. For Christian pupils 'Rites restore, reinforce or redirect indentity ... they unify, integrate and sacralize'. Rites represent sameness of action and thereby consolidate the sameness of a system of meaning.[10]

Faith, Culture and the Dual System

Christian worship in a multibelief situation raises crucial questions. The act of Christian worship, while focussing attention upon God, also draws attention to distinctions — (whether they are cultural or religious) — to 'others'. It raises questions about what participation in Christian worship means to non-Christian pupils. Participation may provide a framework for learning and understanding, but for non-Christians it cannot be Christian worship, if the Durham Report's view is accepted that 'worship ... can only be worship if it is indeed the appropriate response of creature to creator and as such an activity undertaken for its own sake'.[11]

If worship requires some commitment and a belief in what is worshipped which pupils do not claim, then do teachers have the right to ask children to affirm a commitment which may not exist? Does the presence of non-Christian pupils highlight imperfections in school worship where the actuality envisaged in drawing up the aims and objectives of school assembly and worship, fails today to coincide with what was originally intended? If this is the case does it result in a misplacement of goals? The multiplicity of religious beliefs represented in church secondary schools has not brought about any questioning of, or reflection on Christian worship in a religiously plural environment.

Drawing on the research we have seen that the range of aims, content and nature of assemblies is much wider in county schools. Non-religious assemblies, however, claim the support in over 55 per cent of county schools. In coping with the exigencies of social situations both church and county schools have opted for different approaches. Formal religion has been marginalized in many county schools' assemblies while it remains at the centre in church schools.

What happens in assembly is a result of selecting on the basis of relevance and merit. Some values are seen as more important than others. It follows that what is omitted is seen either as inappropriate, irrelevant or having a low priority.

The word 'collective' in the 1944 Act implies a concern for school unity and collective worship was seen as an appropriate way of establishing and reinforcing unity. County headteachers point to the difficulties in providing a collective act of worship which will provide an appropriate communal experience for the school community. Today many county school assemblies are seen as a logical extension of the principles enshrined in the 1944 Act in so far as they foster the school spirit. Assemblies are directed at the development of a unified school community in which over-arching values and norms play a central role. Such assemblies provide fewer opportunities for preparing children for 'the life of the imagination'[12] and to foster a sense of the numinous.

School Worship and Assemblies

Glock and Stark outline five ways in which religion is expressed and they provide a useful sociological description for looking at school worship. These dimensions are (i) the ideological dimension which encompasses the religious beliefs held by adherents; (ii) the ritualistic dimension which involves the specific practices and religious rites, for example, prayer, worship and sacraments; (iii) the experiential dimension which relates to the subjective religious experience and emotion; (iv) the intellectual dimension is closely related to the ideological dimension and involves an understanding and knowledge of the basic doctrines of faith; and (v) the consequential dimension concerns 'the secular effects of religious belief, practice, experience and knowledge on the individual . . . In the language of Christian belief, the consequential dimension deals with man's relation to man . . .'.[13] In over half the county schools in the study, the ritualistic and experiential dimensions of religion discussed in theory in the religious education class will not be given practical expression in the school. The act of school worship is not seen as having an educative role. There is an underlying assumption that if the commitment school worship presupposes does not exist, then school worship is inappropriate. In church schools all Glock and Stark's dimensions are present in the life of the school as far as Christian children are concerned but they are in many cases absent for non-Christian children. The act of school worship in church schools can be described as 'religious observance' for Christian children but 'religious observation' for non-Christian children where their religion is invisible and confined to a private sphere within the school.

The majority of county and church schools separate faith from culture and in doing so they fragment the essential wholeness or unity of human life. In an attempt to strip assembly and school worship of all ambiguity most county schools have adopted a cultural response where the religious essence has escaped or been removed intentionally, abandoning the religious element in favour of that which is secular. In such a situation the religious dimension becomes a private affair.

The School Council Report on Religious Education summarizes the fundamental principles of cultural pluralism that have relevance to our discussion on school assemblies and school worship. They point to an ideology based on minority groups' participation in a just society; equal rights with the majority and a cultural status for all. The attitude to religion is based on an 'interactional approach' with the principles of 'religious variability'; the celebration of diversity; mutual enrichment and the 'notion of religious evolution'. The approach adopted in many county schools is more in character with an approach described by the Schools Council as 'separatism'. They summarize the features of this approach as an 'avoidance of conflict'; where 'religion is a private matter for the individual and minority cultures'.[14]

John McIntyre in discussing educational responses to multicultural and multifaith issues makes an important point: 'It is quite unhistorical and distortive to extract the religion from the cultural presentation as if it were an expendable extra; and equally misrepresentative of the religion in each case to regard it as occurring in some kind of cultural vacuum'.[15] Both church and county schools are guilty of this distortion.

By their omission, school assemblies which can find no time for ritual or give expression to the sacred or transcendent manifest an ethic which places a low value on the collective spiritual or religious dimension to life.

I want to conclude this chapter by raising a number of issues and challenges facing church schools. First, in accepting pupils from non-Christian homes, the schools, and thereby the church, are committed to develop to the full, the potential of all pupils. If schools neglect the religious experience, beliefs and traditions of children of other faiths, can it be said that in this sense, it is a case of the church being concerned primarily with its own followers? Second, does school worship in church schools reduce dialogue between Christians and other faiths to a purely one-way process? Third, the challenge for church schools today is two-fold. On the one hand, there remains a demand for bearing witness to a Christian way of life. On the other hand, how to respond to the challenge which pupils of other faiths present to Christians. These issues and challenges highlight the need to explore theologically areas that include the nature and aims of worship in a community of mixed beliefs. K. Cracknell and C. Lamb raise important questions for church schools, 'What is the proper form for a school assembly in a multi-religious school? or even in an all-white school which wishes to be sensitive to the multi-religious society it is part of? How can the integrity of every conscience be respected while introducing children to the fundamentals of worship?'[16]

Notes

1 *Education Act (1944)*, section 25 (1).
2 *Ibid*, section 26.
3 The National Association of Headteachers, at the annual conference in 1983, asked its Council to establish a working party to consider possible revisions of section 25 of the 1944 Education Act and to report its findings to the conference in 1984. The working party was set up and recommendations were made calling for changes in the wording of the act which would

provide a legal basis for school worship to be held less frequently and delegating the responsibility to governors in consultation with the head of each school 'to determine the nature frequency of acts of worship'.

The National Union of Teachers in their document *Religious Education in a Multifaith Society* point out that many teachers see daily worship (presumably Christian) harmful to the spirit of multicultural education.

4 Department of Education and Science (1985) *Education for All. The Report of the Committee of Enquiry into the Education of Children from Ethnic Minority Groups* (The Swann Report), Cmnd 9453, London, HMSO, p. 773.
5 I have used these broad categories which were used by Souper and Kay in the School Assembly in Hampshire. See SOUPER P.C. and KAY W.K. (1982) *Report of a Pilot Study*, School Assembly Project Working Paper Two, Southampton, University of Southampton, Department of Education. Although administrative matters were often dealt with at assemblies, they were not, however, considered a main aim.
6 M. RUTTER *et al.*, have made an important contribution in this area. See RUTTER, M. *et al.*, (1979) *Fifteen Thousand Hours; Secondary Schools and Their Effects on Children*, London, Open Books.
7 DANCY, J. (1980) 'Perspectives I', in the *Rutter Research*, Exeter, University of Exeter, School of Education, pp. 29–37.
8 NICHOLS, K. (1979) *Orientations. Six Essays on Theology and Education*, St. Paul Publications, p. 23.
9 *The Fourth R*, (1972), The Durham Report on Religious Education, National Society SPCK, p. 134.
10 MOL, H. (1976) *Identification and the Sacred*, Oxford, Basil Blackwell, p. 233.
11 *The Fourth R* (1972) *op. cit.*, p. 136.
12 WARNOCK, M. (1978) 'The Good Life', section III, *Schools of Thought*, Faber and Faber.
13 STARK, R. and GLOCK, C.Y. (1965) *Religion and Society in Tension* Chicago, Rand McNally p. 18.
14 WOOD, A. *Assessment in a Multicultural Society: Religious Studies at 16+*, Schools Council Programme 5, Improving the Examination System.
15 McINTYRE, J. *Multiculture and Multifaith Societies: Some Examinable Assumptions*. Occasional Papers No. 3, The Farmington Institute for Christian Studies.
16 CRACKNELL, K. and LAMB, C. (1984) *Theology on Full Alert*, British Council of Churches, p. 17.

Chapter 6

Religious Education

The 1944 Education Act made the teaching of religion a legal requirement in all schools:

> Religious Instruction shall be given in every county school and every voluntary school. (section 25.1)

The Act also made provision for parents to withdraw their children from religious instruction on religious grounds.

Nowhere in the Act is it specified what religion was to be taught but at the time there was a general consensus that pupils would be instructed in the Christian faith in a society that was seen as Christian.

The 1944 Education Act thus provides the basis for Christian nurture in county schools and denominational nurture in church voluntary schools. Nurture took the form of the imparting of knowledge of the Bible, instruction in, and practice of, the Christian faith.

Forty years later, the religious clauses embodied in the Act remain without amendment and its legacy must be faced. Many of the changes that have taken place in society since its enactment have had a direct effect upon the teaching of religious education. Within the classroom there has been a movement away from traditional religious instruction based on the Christian faith to new models of religious education which include the study of world religions and 'other stances' for living.

The Birmingham Agreed Syllabus demonstrates not only the move away from Christian nurture but the justification of religious education based on educational principles:

> A generation ago the purpose of religious education in county schools was to nurture pupils into Christian faith ... In the present circumstances religious education is seen as an educationally valid component of the school curriculum, subject to

Faith, Culture and the Dual System

the same disciplines as any other area of study. It is thus directed towards developing a critical understanding of the religious and moral dimensions of human experience and away from attempting to foster the claims of particular religious standpoints.

It became evident that not all schools in the study conform with the legal requirement of providing religious education for all pupils. The following table provides details of RE provision in secondary schools.

TABLE 26: *Percentage distribution of religious education provision in county and church secondary schools*

	Provision	
	County	Church secondary
	(percentage in brackets)	
Forms 1–6	4 (14.2)	12 (31.6)
Forms 1–5 Optional 6th form	6 (21.3)[1]	21 (55.2)[3]
Forms 1–5 General Studies 6th form	2 (7.0)	3 (8.0)
Forms 1–3	13 (47.0)[2]	2 (5.2)
Forms 1–6 Social Education	1 (3.5)	–
Forms 1–5 R.E. part of Humanities	1 (3.5)	–
Forms 1–2	1 (3.5)	–
Total	28 (100.0)	38 (100.0)

Notes:
1 In one school, only a minority of pupils in form 5 attend RE classes which are timetabled at the same time as games and PE.
2 In two schools RE classes are optional.
3 Four church schools have been included where pupils study for their 'A' levels at a sixth form centre.

Table 26 shows that religious education through the age range is provided in four (14 per cent) county schools and twelve (31 per cent) church schools. In the majority of these schools RE is either optional or not provided for sixth-form pupils.

In just under half the county schools, and in one church school, pupils in fourth and fifth forms receive no religious education. In addition, one county school provides religious education for first and second year pupils only. In a further two county schools RE is

Religious Education

TABLE 27: *Cross-tabulation of the number of secondary schools and incidence of religious education lessons per week*

	One lesson	Two lessons	Three lessons	Four lessons	Five lessons	Optional/ none	%
Form 1							
Church	1	32	4	–	–	–	97
County	14	13	–	–	–	–	96
Form 2							
Church	2	33	3	–	–	–	100
County	12	14	–	–	–	(1)	93
Form 3							
Church	6	28	3	–	1	–	100
County	14	11	–	–	–	(2)	93
Form 4							
Church	5	12	12	7	1	(1)	97
County	10	1	3	1	–	(13)	54
Form 5							
Church	6	12	5	10	3	(2)	95
County	10	2	2	1	–	(13)	54
Form 6							
Church	1	–	27	1	1	(8)	79
County	4	–	6	1	–	(17)	39

Notes:
1 The category optional/none is excluded from percentage calculation
2 In fifteen church schools there is no RE provision for non 'A'-level pupils
3 Four church schools send pupils to sixth-form colleges as they have no sixth-form
4 Figures for forms 1, 2, and 3 reflect a pupil intake for one county school commencing age 14+ and one church school commencing 12+

integrated with social studies and humanities courses which are linked to moral, health and careers education.

RE teachers provided details of the number of weekly lessons provided for pupils. In schools where pupils are provided with one double period per week this has been recorded as two lessons.

As table 27 shows, in county schools the number of RE lessons decrease for the older pupils except when pupils are being prepared for CSE, 'O' level and 'A' level examinations. With the exception of three county schools all first, second and third year pupils are provided with at least one RE lesson a week and approximately half these schools provide two lessons a week. Sixteen county schools enter pupils for CSE and 'O' level examinations and in seven schools pupils are prepared for 'A' level examinations.

The majority of church schools provide at least two RE lessons a week for all pupils up to the sixth form. In three schools, however, RE classes are optional for fourth form pupils in one school and in another two schools they are optional for fifth form pupils.

Faith, Culture and the Dual System

The increase in the number of lessons provided for fourth, fifth and sixth form pupils is linked to the fact that in thirty-seven church schools pupils are entered for CSE and 'O' level examinations. Twenty-seven schools also enter pupils for 'A' level examinations.

In each of the three county schools where RE is integrated with social studies and the humanities course practice differs. In one school where RE is taught as part of the humanities course it is integrated with geography, English and history and, it is also part of a community education course. In the second school the RE teacher stressed that 'pupils do not have lessons that are specifically RE instead one period a week is spent on social education which includes health, sex, RE, morals and careers education. In the third school, RE forms part of the social education course'. The RE teacher commented — 'All the major world religions are described so that pupils may understand and respect the faiths of others ... No periods are timetabled as RE at any stage of the school. RE is part of the social education course.'

In schools where religious education provision was limited to the lower forms, teachers noted a lack of pupil demand, lack of staff and organizational factors. Furthermore, adverse effects on its subject status occurred when RE was optional.

Regarding the standing of RE in schools, RE teachers were asked — what is the status of RE in the school curriculum? A summary of their replies is given in table 28.

TABLE 28: *Status of RE in the school curriculum*

	County	Church secondary
	(percentage in brackets)	
High	7 (25)	25 (66)
High up to 'A' levels	—	2 (5)
Fairly high	2 (7)	3 (8)
Needs building up	2 (7)	1 (3)
Low but improving	4 (14)	3 (8)
Low/very low	13 (47)	4 (10)
Total	28 (100)	38 (100)

In two county schools with high status RE the subject is integrated with social studies.

That high status is often a result of careful planning and staff cooperation became evident as the following extract shows:

> The staff have agreed to work cooperatively. The RE syllabus has an agreed status which means it has been thrashed out among the staff. We see it as part of our role to provide this dimension to education. The social education course has a high

Religious Education

status. It is run by the Deputy Head, myself and six other members of the staff. It has lavish provision.

It is useful to link the provision of RE in just under half the county schools, for first, second and third year pupils only, with the incidence of low status RE.

Surprisingly, however, only twenty-five (66 per cent) RE teachers in church schools said that RE had a high status despite the central place afforded to Christianity in the life of the school. Within this group three teachers qualified their answers. In one school although RE has high status 'it is under attack to reduce the time allocated to RE for computer studies'. Another teacher points to insufficient time allocated to RE 'while it has a high profile it has the lowest percentage of time for any CSE and 'O' level subject'. Another RE teacher said 'Our school is being constantly secularized. We have too many staff who are not Christians'.

The main factors that contribute to the status of RE are mentioned in the RE teachers' remarks given below. Status depends on whether it is a core subject in the curriculum, if there is a general consensus among staff concerning its status and whether it is an externally examined subject:

> It is accepted as part of their commitment when pupils come into the school. It is on a par with other subjects and it is an examined subject. It is part of the core curriculum which gives it dignity and status, otherwise it would have to fight for its survival if it were an option. As a Christian foundation it is central.

Another teacher mentioned the importance of commitment:

> The whole ethos in the past and present is Christian-based. RE is an extension of this. A lot of the staff are actively committed church folk and are teaching their subjects in a Christian way.

In addition to staff, parents play a key role in determining the status of religious education in the school. A county teacher illustrates this point:

> RE has a low status, especially in the eyes of the staff. More importantly, parents also see it as a low status subject. The younger kids are OK but they tend to be put off by the image of RE and this image is given to them largely by their parents who think it is a waste of time.

Another county teacher commented:

> There is a gulf between teachers. RE is fine as a subject until the

pupils are faced with a choice of 'A' level, then many teachers consider it a soft option and advise against.

In church schools there is often a gulf between what is seen as the ideal and as the reality of the situation. In schools where RE has a low status it is often competing for a greater share in the timetable.

RE has a very low profile in the school curriculum. I was disappointed and ashamed when I came that in a C of E school it had such a low profile. When I tried to introduce extra time for RE they thought it was too much. If we do change to a forty period week we might have two lessons all the way through the school for RE.

Other RE teachers in church schools made comments along the following lines. 'RE is a scale 2 — Cinderella salary — scalewise Cinderella salary — scalewise Cinderella subject; no status; teachers in general do not give it much prestige; RE has the lowest percentage time in the timetable allowed for any 'O' level and CSE level.'

The statutory right of parents to withdraw their children from religious education is exercised in county schools. In sixteen (57 per cent) county schools pupils withdraw from RE classes. In fifteen of these schools pupils sit in class with set work to do. Non-Christian pupils, particularly Muslims, withdraw in ten schools and in seven of these schools, Jehovah's Witnesses also withdraw.

When asked to comment on the reasons for withdrawals in the remaining school the RE teacher said 'It's usually children who are skivving who do not want to do the subject and their parents usually collaborate with them because they think RE is a waste of time.'

Overall, however, the fact emerges that only a very small percentage of the total number of pupils belonging to non-Christian faiths withdraw from religious education classes in county schools.

Pupils withdraw from religious education in only two (5 per cent) church secondary schools. RE teachers' remarks on withdrawals revealed that very few pupils ask to withdraw. Parents were told when applying for a place for their child that RE and school worship were compulsory for pupils. Comments that highlighted this point included — 'No opting out here. They know the situation when they come to the school'; 'rules of the school'. In one church school the RE teacher mentioned that many of the pupils found it difficult to take RE seriously. Pupils were not interested and thought it an irrelevant subject. This teacher recalled the situation when she took up her post — 'The pupils

Religious Education

could not believe I was going to make them work. Before, it was heels on the desks and chewing gum!'

In order to discover the aims and objectives of RE, teachers' views were sought. Open-ended questions were posed so as not to restrict answers.

The following table summarizes RE teachers' replies in secondary schools to the question — as a result of RE what do you hope to achieve for pupils by the time they leave school?

TABLE 29: *RE teachers' replies in secondary schools to the question — as a result of RE what do you hope to achieve for pupils by the time they leave school?*

Replies	Church	County
	(percentage in brackets)	
Grounding in Christianity	18 (47)	4 (14)
Pupil-centred aims	20 (53)	10 (36)
Society/other-centred aims	9 (24)	13 (46)
Academic knowledge to understand about religion	8 (21)	12 (43)

The categories of responses that have been included under the heading 'Christian grounding' are those replies where the prime focus of attention is on the Christian faith. These replies were expressed in the following way:

> I hope pupils can pose questions on the basis of a solid background of Biblical knowledge.

> To produce people who have a respect for, and who feel that they have a place in the church and who are imbued with a sense of Christian values.

> This is a Christian school and our parents expect us to bring their children up in the Christian faith.

Other responses included — 'I am preparing them for a Christian life-style and a personal and detailed knowledge of Christianity'. Two teachers see their main aim as 'providing a context for an encounter with Christ'. To help interpret the data, the overlap with pupil-centred aims is kept separate as the grounding in Christianity category takes as its starting point the Christian faith, whether it is taught with a view to deepening the commitment of Christian pupils or to enlighten pupils about Christianity.

Under the heading pupil-centred aims are included replies where teachers take as their starting point the pupils' own search for meaning

95

Faith, Culture and the Dual System

and purpose to life and where the quest of the child is seen as central. The responsibility of the teacher is seen as one of assisting pupils in their search. The following two extracts illustrate child-centred aims:

> We hope that they will know what it means to have a faith to live by and we hope that we will be able to give them the tools to find such a faith for themselves.

> I hope they will begin to find their own position in their quest for an understanding to life. To understand the meaning that religion can give to human existence.

These teachers often quoted the Durham Report which states 'The aim of religious education should be to explore the place and significance of religion in human life and so make a distinctive contribution to each pupil's search for a faith by which to live.'[1]

As Brenda Watson points out the word 'search' can operate on two different levels. On the one hand pupils can look for explanations and answers to the questions they are raising, 'doubt in its various forms is the handmaid of such enquiry and there are many whose only way forward is through this gateway'. On the other hand, 'it can be thought of as a continuing engagement in the deepening and widening of one's basic convictions; such a search depends upon affirmation and delights in discovering fresh insights derived from the empathetic study of other people's experiences'.[2]

While the above aims are concerned with promoting a religious response the following teacher's comments show that while the aim is still pupil-centred, the personal beliefs of the pupils are not the RE teacher's concern:

> The main aim is to understand the significance that religion can make to human life and experience. How religion can affect the whole of someone's life. I am not trying to turn out good Anglicans, but to show them that a religious outlook on life is still a viable option in the twentieth century. I want them to think about ultimate questions.

These replies support much of the current thinking on religious education, which sees the main aims of exploring the nature of religion in terms of beliefs, practices and interpretation, rather than one of establishing or even nurturing faith.

The heading 'academic knowledge' covers replies that place the main emphasis on 'teaching facts about religion; to inform; to provide pupils with the 'basic information' and the 'intellectual tools to study religion'. The following extracts are typical of the replies in this group:

> The main aim is to acquire a reasonable knowledge about world religions, including knowledge about Christianity. It is important to understand the latter because this has underpinned English culture and tradition.

In addition, aims are closely linked with examinations:

> A clear objective is to get pupils through the CSE. That is one way of raising the status of the subject. Also one of my aims is to get them to have an open mind about religion, to argue from knowledge rather than ignorance.

A church school teacher also highlights the influence of examinations on the teaching of RE — 'My main aim is for pupils to pass exams. We are initially teachers as opposed to missionaries, so exams figure high on the agenda.'

Two observations can be made about RE teachers' replies in this group. First, religion is presented as an academic subject and not as a possible source of faith. Second, these teachers in moving away from the traditional aim of nurture have adopted a stance that reflects the view that 'RE teachers are learning to think more as educators, and less as catechists or evangelists'.[3]

Aims that did not include the pupil's personal search for meaning but sought to dispel ignorance and create tolerance towards others have been grouped under 'society or other-centred' aims. Just under half the county RE, and just under a quarter of church RE teachers mentioned these aims. The starting point is other faiths, other cultures or views. The following three extracts from interviews illustrate this 'otherness':

> The main aim is the understanding of other peoples, particularly other races' points of view and an understanding of other faiths. We had some persecution of girls here, for example, an Indian girl worshipping a monkey [sic] was ridiculed. I introduced the story where the monkey was seen as a hero and that stopped it.

> To start tolerating each others' views. It is particularly important in this area where we have many different cultures. Children are quick to make racist remarks but once they begin to understand different cultures they will get along better and be less prejudiced.

Faith, Culture and the Dual System

And finally,

> In this area we have a large Asian community and there is a lot of intolerance amongst youngsters, possibly gleaned from their parents. We hope that they will have an understanding of other faiths, and be more tolerant. I hope that bridges between faiths will be established.

These extracts focus attention on RE and the impact it can have as playing an important role in bringing about changes in attitudes, counteracting misunderstanding and challenging prejudices and stereotypes. In this context the very nature of religious education cannot be passive as it implies taking steps to eliminate racist attitudes and to dismantle harmful stereotypes. The positive approach adopted by these teachers is echoed in Owen Cole's conviction that ... 'religious education has perhaps the greatest contribution to make in educating everyone for a multicultural society'.[4]

Replies already discussed to the question on the aims of religious education provide only a partial picture. RE teachers were asked whether they thought that an aim of religious education is to nurture the personal faith of pupils. It was necessary first, to find out if it was an aim among RE teachers interviewed and second, if they thought that certain school environments were more conducive to nurturing the personal faith of pupils than others. A summary of replies follows:

TABLE 30: *Replies to the question — do you think that an aim of RE is to nurture the personal faith of pupils?*

	Church	County
	(percentage in brackets)	
Yes	26 (69)	13 (46)*
No	8 (21)	13 (46)
Can do, but not an aim	2 (5)	2 (8)
Others — not sure	2 (5)	—
Total	38 (100)	28 (100)

* Included in these statistics are the replies of five county school teachers who said nurture was possible in church schools but not in county schools.

It is clear from these statistics that it can no longer be assumed that nurture has a place in religious education in 31 per cent of church schools and in 71 per cent of county schools. Some replies to the question revealed a confusion over the word 'nurture'. 'My answer is yes, but I am not sure that it is what we are allowed to do by law.' Another said, 'Yes, it is an aim but one could be accused of indoctrination.' Both these comments were from county RE teachers. Five county teachers accepted that nurture was possible in a church school but not in a county school. 'If I was teaching in a church school, then it would definitely be an aim. In a county school the RE teacher is not there to nurture.' However, one RE teacher in a church school said 'It is much easier in Roman Catholic schools — their schools are for Catholic children. Our schools have to cope with materialist youngsters from materialist homes.'

Teachers who do not see nurture as one of their aims answered in terms of strictly educational RE. Teachers in church schools who have abandoned nurture had moved away from the domestic aim of the church school in fostering the Christian faith. It is clear that crucial questions arise in these schools particularly where the act of worship is seen as affirmation, faith-assuming and faith-nurturing.

Another RE teacher in a church school opposing nurture as an aim said, 'Most pupils do not have a personal faith. It is the job of the Church. The school is not a pew-filler for the Church of England. Religious studies is an academic subject. We teach Biblical truths.' While many would want to question the validity of religious studies as an academic subject when it aims to impart 'Biblical truths', it is more difficult to make sense of this statement in the light of the fact that this school is a popular over-subscribed school where 85 per cent of the pupils come from Christian homes. Perhaps what this teacher is implying is that even young people from Christian backgrounds possess secular outlooks.

Other RE teachers who could no longer accept nurture as an aim of religious education linked their replies to the religious diversity of pupils' backgrounds and frequently these teachers posed the question — how is it possible to nurture the faiths of pupils when there is such diversity? Their replies highlighted a pragmatic response devoid of any theological rationale in responding to teaching in multifaith situations.

In 69 per cent of church schools Christian nurture continues to be an important aim. RE teachers in these schools see their activities as making a distinctive contribution to Christian growth. That is not to say that these activities are restricted to church schools only. Similar views were expressed by 29 per cent of RE teachers in county schools.

Two county school RE teachers see Christian voluntary groups as providing an opportunity for faith nurture. One teacher discussing a Christian voluntary group which meets during lunchtime explained, 'There are many parents who want Christian teaching and my sympathies are with them. We have a Christian Fellowship group that meets during the lunch hours. These meetings enable pupils to grow in their faith and my role is to help them strengthen their faith.' The other

Faith, Culture and the Dual System

teacher distinguished between the school providing nurture in religious education classes and in voluntary Christian groups. 'We have a Christian club for those that want to attend and it is made quite clear that those attending want to embrace Christianity. In the classroom RE Christianity is really taught as an historical faith that is alive today. A minority of RE teachers in church schools also referred to the importance of Christian voluntary groups.

The ambiguity surrounding nurture became more evident when considering teachers' views on the statement — 'religious education that is concerned with nurturing and teaching for commitment within a community of faith is justified because the child is better able to understand other religions'. This statement concerns both principle and practice. It is not assumed that it is the sole justification but possibly one justification among others. The RE teachers' views are given in the following table:

TABLE 31: RE teachers' view on the statement — RE that is concerned with Christian nurturing and teaching for commitment is justified within a Community of faith because the child is better able to understand other religions

	Church	County
	(percentage in brackets)	
Agree	22 (58)	9 (32)
Disagree	9 (24)	15 (54)
Not sure	7 (18)	4 (14)
Total	38 (100)	28 (100)

Expressing a view on this statement proved to be a difficult task for many teachers and they tackled the problem from different angles. Some teachers did not accept the premise that Christian nurturing and teaching for commitment were justified in schools under any circumstances. A number of teachers from both county and church schools responded in this way. Others said that Christian nurturing and teaching for commitment could be justified without any reference to other religions. 'I don't see what understanding of other religions has got to do with it. Christian commitment is of value in itself. Understanding other religions is an incidental bonus.'

The word 'tolerant' was frequently used by teachers who agreed with the statement in the sense that they suggested that pupils who were themselves committed to a religious viewpoint would have a better basis for understanding the 'why' questions central to the religious activities of other religious groups, and therefore they would be more tolerant. Intolerance featured significantly in teachers' replies who took the opposite view. A county teacher commented:

Religious Education

If anything, pupils will be more intolerant. They would be much more likely to conclude that other religions are wrong.

A church school teacher said:

I disagree with the statement. I don't see why it should make them better able to understand other religions. If anything it will create a prejudiced point of view.

Other teachers pointed out, if you nurture in one faith you might not do justice to other religions.

The point of immediate relevance here is that these comments reveal the importance of the approach adopted by RE teachers. Teachers have a responsibility to ensure that pupils do not become prejudiced or intolerant as a result of their teaching methods. As one county teacher commented — 'what is important is the approach that is adopted. If during your teaching you impress on a child that Christianity is the only true religion or superior to other religions, then the child may become intolerant to other faiths'. The crucial link is between what is being taught and the manner in which it is taught.

The two aspects of the statement involve both educational concerns and religious commitment concerns. For teachers who disagreed with the statement these two aspects existing side by side are incompatible. There is no recognition of nurture having a legitimate place in religious education classes in addition to education. To take this view is to deny that the teacher can also be concerned with education. Another key point is that considerable confusion is engendered by the concept of nurture. Some see it as 'the closest you can get to indoctrination'; others see it as indoctrination and a 'closedness'. Indeed for these teachers there is no middle ground between education and indoctrination.

A great deal of attention has been given to the place of Christianity in religious education classes. While it continues to find a place in all schools in the study it is no longer seen to be the cornerstone of religious education in all schools. While Christianity continues to hold a central place in thirty-six (95 per cent) church schools only sixteen (53 per cent) RE teachers in county schools said it remains the cornerstone of religious teaching. Where it exists the major reason given for the centrality of Christianity in county schools reflects the Schools Council's view that:

The tradition of our national life has been largely shaped and sustained by behaviour and ideas closely associated with the practice of religion, and particularly the Christian religion. Since education involves a thorough exploration of the environ-

Faith, Culture and the Dual System

ment and the received culture, this source of our national heritage should be studied and appreciated. An investigation of religion and its claims is thus an important part of education in Britain, whether the pupils have any religious affiliation or not.[5]

In addition a small minority of teachers said that Christianity holds a central place for practical reasons. A county RE teacher's reply illustrates this point. 'It is purely because I myself know more about Christianity and I am still trying to learn about other religions'. Another said 'Yes it tends to be mainly for practical reasons. A lot of the materials we have are geared towards Christianity.'

In county schools where Christianity is not accorded a central place, the two reasons, although often related, are linked to the diversity of faiths in the schools. Firstly, as one teacher points out 'A multifaith emphasis does not allow for any of the competing religions in the school to have priority'. The second reason concerns the lack of time allocation to religious education. A county teacher described the situation in his school. 'In the first year it is a thematic approach. In the second and third years we devote half a year to each of the four religions. In the second year we look at Islam and Hinduism and in the third year we look at Buddhism and Christianity.' This was the complete religious education for the whole of the pupils secondary school education. This type of situation was by no means an isolated occurrence.

Generally speaking, a recurring theme is evident in the RE teachers replies in church schools. For them, Christianity is more than a timetable subject. It is not simply a cultural heritage to be studied for purely historical reasons. Instead Christianity is a living faith and church schools are involved in witnessing the Christian faith and contributing to the Christian growth of pupils. Their replies echoed the view expressed in the Camberwell Papers that a central concern is 'to enable the pupils to understand Christianity and see the Christian faith applied'.

In addition, twenty-one (55 per cent) RE teachers in church schools said that religious education is centred on the 'Church of England teachings'. In just under a quarter of church schools, pupils are prepared for confirmation.

In order to find out whether religious education is seen as providing a basis for Christian morality RE teachers were asked the following question-'as a result of RE do you hope that pupils will have a clear understanding of Christian morality?'. The following table summarizes replies to that question.

As one would expect, teachers who said that Christianity was not

Religious Education

TABLE 32: *RE teachers' replies to the question — as a result of RE do you hope that pupils will have a clear understanding of christian morality?*

	Church	County
	(percentage in brackets)	
Yes	37 (97)	19 (68)[1]
No	1 (3)	6 (21)
Not necessarily Christian morality	—	3 (11)
Total	38 (100)	28 (100)

Note: Two teachers in this group qualified their replies by saying that pupils' understanding of Christian morality would be no greater than Hindu or Jewish morality

the cornerstone of religious education did not see education as providing the basis for Christian morality. One teacher expressed this view in the following way:

> No this is not a top priority. It doesn't matter if we do Christianity, Islam or Hinduism. I can't see that an inner city school in London being concerned with Christianity is a central thing.

This viewpoint is a departure from that expressed by E. Durkheim, the French sociologist who spoke of the teacher as 'the interpreter of great moral ideas of his time and country'.[6]

Another teacher distinguishes between Christian morality and morality in general:

> No, not specifically Christian morality but perhaps morality in general. Certainly, I am not trying to get them to see things from a Christian standpoint or to look upon moral issues with only a Christian attitude. There is also a secular moral attitude and this is the one that they will come into contact with most in the world.

It is difficult to envisage how pupils in these schools can have a clear understanding and be able to make informed decisions about religion when Christianity can be studied without thorough attention to the content of morality, what constitutes moral action or, indeed, without being aware that religion entails morality. Table 32 shows that the majority of RE teachers see religious education as providing the basis for understanding Christian morality. However, in six (21 per cent) county schools and in one church school this is not a priority.

In general, RE teachers in church schools link the teaching of Christian morality to the whole ethos of the school:

Faith, Culture and the Dual System

> A clear understanding of morality is essential. We try to make this a Christian school. The whole ethos is that you are an individual and you are cared for. We want you to use your talents that God has given you in God's world.

Another said:

> I would hope their view of Christian morality would come from all subjects, not just RE. This is a Christian school and Christian morality fuses all of the school. Assembly is a particularly important place for putting forward Christian morality.

The Christian context was also mentioned by a small number of teachers in county schools. One county RE teacher commented that 'morals cannot be taught in a vacuum. Here they have a Christian context.'

Some teachers in county and church schools who hoped pupils would have a clear understanding of Christian morality linked the answers to their own personal faith as the following comments from county teachers show:

> Yes I hope they will have an understanding of Christian morality. I am a Christian and therefore my moral values will come over. We look at the life of Jesus and what he believed ... In the sixth form we look at social issues like marriage, abortion etc. and consider how a Christian would respond.

> Yes I hope so, otherwise it is all in vain. If as a Christian, I cannot impart an understanding of Christian morality then I have failed in my responsibility.

RE teachers in secondary schools were asked to provide details concerning specific provision for the study of religions other than Christianity. These statistics are provided in the following table:

TABLE 33: Specific provision for the study of world religions in secondary schools

Provision	Church	County
	(percentage in brackets)	
Form 1 only	3 (8)	1 (3)
Form 2 only	3 (8)	5 (18)
Form 3 only	7 (17)	1 (3)
Forms 1–2	3 (8)	–
Forms 1–3	3 (8)	8 (29)
Forms 1–4	1 (3)	1 (3)
Forms 1–5	2 (5)	2 (6)
Forms 1–6	1 (3)	3 (10)

TABLE 33: Continued

Forms 2–5	1 (3)	–
Forms 4–6	2 (5)	2 (6)
Forms 2 and 3 only	2 (5)	1 (3)
Forms 2 and 6	1 (3)	–
Forms 3 and 6 only	1 (3)	–
Forms 4 and 5 only	2 (5)	1 (3)
No specific provision	6 (16)	3 (10)
Total	38 (100)	28 (100)

In a third of church secondary schools and a quarter of county schools the teaching of world religions other than Christianity is confined to forms 1, 2 or 3 only. In county schools specific provision for teaching world religions is more evenly spread throughout the whole school. While the statistics indicate that county schools are providing more time for the study of world religions, this picture is modified as county school pupils have fewer lessons than pupils in church schools.

Table 33 shows that in a third of church schools and a quarter of county schools the study of world religions is confined to a period of one year at the early stages of secondary school education. The question arises — to what extent is the study of world religions perceived by RE teachers as 'tolerated extras'. Clearly in these schools, the multifaith approach advocated by W. Cole has not been adopted. For W. Cole the approach in a multifaith school is outlined in the following way. 'First, the multifaith element will be present from the beginning. There can be no debate when to introduce material from Islam when there are Muslims in the class. Secondly, the multifaith element must pervade every theme or topic as far as is possible. You cannot say to a secondary class "Christianity this year and next — but we do Islam for a term in form 3."'[7] Furthermore, six (16 per cent) church schools and three (10 per cent) county schools' religious education classes have a Christian content only.

It is likely that in schools where the study of world religions other than Christianity is very restricted it is difficult for pupils to arrive at a mature understanding of the religious beliefs, practices and complexities of the different world religions. In most of these schools, at least two world religions will be covered within a period of one year. Indeed, it is very difficult for pupils to listen, understand and evaluate what the religions being studied are really saying when the study of world religions is nothing more than a swift tour with no halting place.

During our research attempts were made to explore the factors governing the selection of world religions for study and we found that in many secondary schools the study of world religions within the religious education class does not take into account the faiths represented in the school. When teachers were asked whether the religions studied reflected the faiths of pupils, fourteen (50 per cent) religious education teachers in county schools said yes. Out of the twenty-one church schools that have non-Christian children only five RE teachers said that the religions studied reflected the different faiths of pupils.

Schools which did endeavour to relate the context of religious education to their pupils' backgrounds did so in a planned way. Background information was collected and on the basis of this information syllabuses were adapted accordingly. One RE teacher in a church school describes this approach:

> Yes, we did a survey a few years ago and we found we have a large number of Hindus in the school but very few other faiths, so we changed our Christian-based syllabus to include Hinduism. We now concentrate on Christianity and Hinduism and we also cover Judaism and Islam in a minor way.

During discussions with RE teachers concerning the teaching of world religions there was, once again, considerable evidence of a lack of understanding and knowledge about world religions. I have compiled a number of extracts which have been included at the end of this chapter, for now, one extract from an interview with a county RE teacher will demonstrate the point: —

> In the second and third year we look at Islam, Buddhism and Judaism. I tend to lump together Taoism and Confucionism if there is time, and if you can call them religions. We might also look at Hinduism which completely baffles me. I think it has hundreds of Gods but Hindus themselves claim that it has the most single God.

The RE teacher who made this comment was originally qualified as a religious education teacher and he has been teaching in the present school for thirty-one years without any in-service training. For teachers who lack the training to teach their subject in a changing context in-service training becomes an urgent necessity. The Swann Report in stressing the importance of in-service training states 'nevertheless, we believe that in-service training has a major role to play in helping all teachers wherever they teach to fulfil their professional responsibilities more effectively' (p. 576).

The reasons given for not relating the content of religious education to the background of pupils were often concerned with pragmatic issues or emphasized subject-centred considerations rather than pupil-centred concerns. The following abstract demonstrates this point:

> It is my policy to stick to three religions — Christianity, Judaism and Islam. However, there are no practising Jews in the school and only one practising Muslim. My reasons for choosing these three religions are, Christianity emerged out of Judaism — it is almost impossible to teach one without the other and Islam has the largest number of adherents.

In one church school where Christianity was the only religion studied the RE teacher intended to extend the syllabus to include five world religions for study in the following year. The five were chosen for the following reasons:

> I have decided on five religions — Christianity, Judaism, Sikhism, Islam and Hinduism but they will not necessarily reflect the faiths of pupils. My reasons for their inclusion is that all of these religions hold that man has a soul [sic] and that is why I have left out Buddhism.

Another teacher in a church school found there was opposition when she introduced world religions and she commented 'I think it is essential if only to avoid unintentional rudeness'.

There are other schools in which RE teachers found it impossible to cover all 'relevant' religions because of the sheer diversity of the religious backgrounds of pupils.

In county schools, the lack of time allocated to religious education with attendent timetabling constraints especially when confined to the first three years was an important consideration when the RE syllabus was seen to have failed to adapt to reflect adequately a diverse pupil composition. Generally speaking church schools allocate more time to religious education but there is little evidence to show that changes are taking place concerning the content of these classes in response to multi-religious situations.

Teachers pointed out that while they include religions for study it is sometimes impossible to do justice to them. Often the time allowed only enables the teacher to 'scatch the surface or to look at the "externalities" of religions.'

In response to the question — do you think children of different faiths should be taught by teachers professing the same faiths — thirteen (34 per cent) teachers in church schools and four teachers (14 per cent) in county schools thought it was a good idea. Teachers in favour gave two main reasons. First, the pupil would benefit and, second, to compensate for the present lack of knowledge on the part of teachers, and for their being on the outside.

> Yes I think in all fairness to the child I think it would be a good idea. Muslims are anxious about Christians teaching their faith because they are not on the inside. As an RE teacher I don't think I could ever do justice to other faiths and nurture children in their own faith.

Another RE teacher said:

> Ideally, yes, I don't think I could ever teach Islam as it should be taught.

Several teachers in county schools distinguished between education and instruction — 'one wonders if there is any openness in a procedure which is instruction rather than education'. Others said religious education must be concerned with an objective study of, and not instruction in religion — 'any teacher can teach religion providing he or she explains the facts'.

Some of the questions concerning children of non-Christian faiths were not seen as relevant by many RE teachers in church schools where the majority of pupils were Christians. Likewise for a smaller number of county schools. In such schools responses were received along the lines 'I can't really comment' or 'the problem doesn't arise here'. This viewpoint was developed by two RE teachers in church schools. 'There are no adherents of other faiths in the school. I haven't got first-hand experience of the situation so I really can't answer.' The other RE teacher said 'People are loathe to do something unless people of other faiths are actually in their midst'.

Attempting to relate RE classes to the faiths of pupils a church school teacher found it difficult to do justice to the manifestation of pluralism within Christianity itself. 'There are many forms of Christianity represented in the school which I have to neglect especially the West Indian forms of Christianity. It is so difficult to know how to approach this diversity.' The difficulty of coping with the diversity in Christianity was a recurring theme among teachers. Teachers often referred to 'Caribbean Pentecostals' as if there was a single form of Pentecostalism, unaware that it is highly diverse. Gerloff, in discussing the development of black churches in Britain since 1952, points out that there are nine 'theological strands or denominational families of Afro-Caribbean origin in Britain'. He distinguishes three different groups

Religious Education

within the Pentecostal movement, the Trinitarian Pentecostals, the Oneness Pentecostals and the Pentecostals Healing Movement all of which exhibit important differences.[8] Clearly 'Christian pluralism' is a complex area but as Rodger states:

> The fact of 'Christian pluralism' has to be faced squarely within religious education. The alternative is to opt for a particular form of Christianity as the 'correct' one; and so to exclude our pupils from the opportunity for experiencing any educational process by which they move through information to understanding as the basis for their own evaluation. The teacher will almost certainly have views on what Christianity is. It will not be his business to ensure that his pupils come to share them, unless a fair consideration of the evidence persuades them to do so.[9]

It will be useful now to turn to the inclusion of non-religious stances for living in religious education classes and consider their growing interaction. The Schools Council states that '... some of the alternatives to religious faith, such as secular Humanism, Marxism and Maoism deserve the same sympathetic study and attention'.[10] Hull outlines the criteria for the inclusion of non-religious stances in a religious education syllabus. First, the ideology or way of life must explicitly reject religion. Second, it must claim to be a substitute for religion. Third, it must nevertheless exhibit certain characteristics of the religions, such as a theory of history, a total view of man and his destiny and a system of ethics.[11]

Although these criteria are necessary for inclusion, Hull points out they are not sufficient in themselves. Furthermore, 'they must be included in their own right and not as a foil to religion'.

Eleven (39 per cent) county schools featured other stances for living in religious education classes. Five of these schools included at least Humanism and Marxism within the syllabus while the remaining schools included either Marxism or Humanism. Fourteen (37 per cent) church schools also provided for other stances for living. In eight schools both Marxism and Humanism were studied while the remaining six schools included for study either Marxism or Humanism. Four county and three church schools included these stances in the syllabus to prepare pupils for external examinations. However, the main reason for their inclusion was concerned with helping pupils to be informed about non-religious interpretations to life. The teacher's personal life stance was not always subdued as is evident from remarks made by one teacher in a county school:

> We do communism in a very anti-way. Some people see it as a religion but it is not. Once we look at Buddhism and then ask — how do you define religion? You see that it can't be based on God because there is no God under Buddhism.

These comments and the underlying approach to teaching stand in opposition to the 'intellectual discipleship' which the Crowther Report related to inspired teaching.[12]

The reasons for not including non-religious stances fall into three main groups. First, teachers had not given serious thought to the possibility of including them. Second, a lack of time made the study of them impossible. Third, a minority of teachers said they were not considered to be the concern of religious education. This minority view provided evidence to show that attitudes, prejudices and values of RE teachers effect decisions concerning the content of religious education. Two RE teachers, one church and one county, subscribed to the view 'No, other stances are not included. They are not consistent with the teaching of Christ as understood by the church'. One teacher in a church school shows how tension may arise among teachers with differing values. 'Non-religious stances are not covered in religious education but a lot of this goes on with the atheist teachers in the school. I am sad to say that there are too many of these in a church school.' One final comment from a county school teacher shows the impossibility of 'procedural neutrality' as far as he is concerned: 'No they are not included. They are all false stances. The school does not teach erroneous systems of maths or physics either.'

For these teachers, at least, it would appear that despite what has been written on 'neutrality' it still remains a purely intellectual exercise for theorists. In the classroom values continue to impinge in a very significant way.

To sum up at this point, religious education in many schools has changed in varying degrees in its aim and content. It has adapted to its social context by shifting the focus from one centred on Christianity to one which includes the study of world religions and non-religious stances of living. Today, in many schools Christianity is taught alongside other religions. The secular principle is employed in the majority of county schools and a minority of church schools. Its underlying assumption is that it is not the function of the school to commend any one of the competing religions or life stances that exist within society today. As Rodger points out 'If a school positively penalizes a religious or a non-religious outlook or stance for living then it has infringed this basic principle.'[13]

Religious Education

Headteachers in primary schools were asked to provide details of the aims and objectives of religious education in their school. A summary is provided in the following table:

TABLE 34: *Headteachers' replies concerning the aims and objectives of RE in primary schools*

Aims	
Understanding Christianity	32 (84%)
Developing Christian ideals	11 (29%)
Providing awareness that religion is important in later life	8 (21%)
Tolerance of others — especially religious and racial tolerance	7 (18%)

Note: Where teachers gave one or more aims in any one category they have been included under the relevant category. Eleven teachers mentioned more than one aim.

For the majority of headteachers in primary schools the main aim of RE is to provide pupils with an understanding of the Christian Faith. The understanding of Christianity is seen as relevant to all pupils whatever their religious backgrounds.

Teachers' replies placed emphasis on educational matters such as understanding society, and religious concerns, which focus on developing or strengthening the faith of Christian pupils.

This point is illustrated in the following remarks:

> My aim is to enable all pupils to have a basic understanding of Christianity. Pupils of other faiths will be coming into contact with Christianity. They will hear about festivals like Christmas and Easter. Some children in the school will be baptised. These outward forms are important for all pupils — those from committed Christian backgrounds or otherwise. They need to understand what is going on around them. At the end of the primary school experience I hope they will understand that people look to their religion in many situations.

A theme running through most of headteachers' replies is the way the teaching of Christianity is linked closely to developing patterns of good behaviour.

> This school's beliefs are based on God the Father, God the Son and the Holy Spirit and through this children can go and follow the parable of the Good Samaritan.

Another said:

> The principles of the Christian Faith act as a basis for development of a compassionate understanding and tolerance in a rapidly changing world in which children will ultimately take

their place as responsible citizens. We teach them to treat others as you would like them to treat you.

and, finally:

I hope to lead pupils some little way into beginning to understand about Jesus and his life and attitudes in a way in which we ought to try and live together, work together and respect and care for each other.

For these teachers the school environment provides a 'fertile ground' for pupils to explore their own faith. The point was made frequently that teachers must start where the pupils are in the act of exploration, understanding and knowledge of the Christian Faith.

Teachers' views echoed the view stated in the Plowden Report:

Child should be taught to know and love God and to practise in the school community the virtues appropriate to the age and environment.[14]

In all primary schools Christianity is the basis of religious education. The central place accorded to Christianity is based on two main views. First, it is educationally sound to start with Christianity as it is familiar to all pupils. 'Even if pupils do not have an acquaintance with the Christian church, it is still the religion that has shaped our society and it is, therefore, the best possible way into understanding religion.' The second view expressed related to the Trust Deeds of church schools and their distinctive Christian character. This view was stated in the following way: 'Our aim is to educate children according to the principles of the Church of England and therefore religious education classes must be concerned with teaching the Christian Faith.'

In nineteen (51 per cent) primary schools Christianity is the only religion studied. While this is frequently the case in schools where the majority of the pupils come from Christian backgrounds it is also the case in schools with many pupils of non-Christian backgrounds.

In twenty-two (59 per cent) schools headteachers said the content of religious education was Bible-based. In fifteen of these schools, religious education included church teaching, the Lord's Prayer, some information on the sacraments and preparations for confirmation.

In just over half (51 per cent) the primary schools where other faiths are not studied two major reasons were given. First, it is not necessary because there are very few non-Christian pupils.

One headteacher in justifying a totally Christian-based religious education said:

RE is Bible-based. We look at the Old and New Testament. There aren't many children of other faiths here. They know it's a church school with Mass on Thursday. Muslim parents are told this and they still prefer a church school because it takes faith more seriously than a county school where religion is watered down.

The view was not expressed by these teachers that Christian pupils need to understand something about different religions in preparation for secondary school or indeed, for life in a religiously plural society. One teacher said that his school discourages multifaith teaching. Another headteacher in a school where the majority of pupils are Muslims said that while she was prepared to discuss their religion with them she did not want to teach their religion because she 'would be a fool rushing in where angels fear to tread'.

Second, some teachers do not have the confidence to teach other faiths; others are not sure if it is in fact the role of the church school to teach other religions. One teacher in pointing to the lack of teaching expertise commented 'The history of church schools is a history of missed opportunities. A great weakness lies with the staff. They have not been trained to teach religious education and there are not enough people capable of conducting good religious education.' Some of the difficulties mentioned could be overcome if, as the Swann Report suggested, one teacher within the primary took responsibility for curriculum development in religious education (p. 491).

In primary schools where religious education is not confined to the teaching of Christianity teachers take as their starting point the need to prepare all pupils for life in a religiously plural society. Teachers outlined different ways of making religious education relevant to the backgrounds of all the pupils. For one headteacher with a large number of Muslim pupils 'the teachers look for things that bind us together rather than divide us. We tell Muslim and Christian stories and we then discover the common moral elements together.' A popular way of introducing different faiths is through stories and project work. Some of the main themes included in project work are the way in which different families live and worship, the different foods we eat, looking at water and light and what they symbolize.

The majority of primary headteachers give priority to an understanding of the Christian faith. The approach to religious education varies from a personal quest for meaning to teaching for Christian commitment. One headteacher described the former approach in the following way: 'my whole teaching is one of quest. I don't regard it as the

Faith, Culture and the Dual System

role of the church school to provide pew-fodder for the church rather to set the children's feet on the pilgrim's way ... If a child passed through my school and took up the Buddhist Faith I wouldn't turn a hair.' Teaching for Christian commitment was expressed by a headteacher as follows: 'We are seeking a commitment to Christianity and this approach is in line with parents' wishes. It is a church school and this is what parents expect.' In this school all the pupils are from Christian backgrounds. The majority of replies fell somewhere in the middle, where headteachers were concerned to enable pupils to grow in their faith, to help them understand, and nurture the faith of pupils.

One hundred and thirty-nine parents who participated in this study were asked for their views concerning the aims of religious education in church schools. Their replies to the question — as a result of religious education what do you hope this school will achieve for your child by the time he/she leaves school? — which have been grouped under six main headings are provided in the following table:

TABLE 35: Parents' replies to the question — *as a result of religious education what do you hope this school will achieve for your child by the time he leaves school?*

Commitment to Christianity	37
Understanding/knowledge of Christianity	41
Understanding religion. Broad religious understanding including other faiths	33
Provide moral standards for living	43
Very little	14
Other	5

Note: Thirty-four parents expressed more than one aim.

Replies which have been placed under 'commitment to Christianity' include all replies where parents expected the school, or more particularly, religious education classes to 'strengthen Christian commitment'; 'to make Christianity a way of life and not something that is practised on Sundays' and to 'strengthen the faith'. Parents in this group also hoped that the religious values in the home would be maintained or reinforced and that pupils would be encouraged to attend church and Sunday School and participate as members of the worshipping community. For these parents, the church school offers a unique opportunity for bringing together three dimensions of a child's experience: home, school and parish church. As the authors of the Durham Report point out, 'The church school can become an educational community which brings into explicit focus the shared assumptions of parents and teachers, the link with the Church exemplifying the beliefs about the purpose of education which underlies the school's activity.' Furthermore, they point out that 'Real educational benefit can be derived from a situation where the school is able to draw upon influences already at work within the community and bring them to explicit expression'.[15]

Forty-one parents did not explicitly say they wanted the children to be committed to Christianity. They hoped that their children would have a better understanding of Christianity, which was something these parents did not mention of other world religions. Some commented that they were not themselves committed Christians and they hoped the school would contribute to the child's understanding of Christianity.

Twenty-three parents hoped that their children would have a broad religious understanding and, therefore, did not want religious education to be confined to the study of Christianity.

Forty-three parents hoped that religious education classes would provide moral standards for living. These parents did not link their answers to religion. Samples of replies in this group are as follows: 'I hope it gives him a caring outlook to life and moral upbringing'; 'I hope he will have reasoned and sound moral attitudes'; 'RE will give him basic standards for life' and 'I hope it teaches her respect for others'.

Parents spoke of a lack of morality in society and on the whole they looked to religious education to fill this moral vacuum. Parents' replies suggest that for them religious education and moral education are closely related. By implication parents consider that the content of religious education will be concerned with morality. Schools are seen as providing 'a code of good behaviour' and obedience to certain rules and desirable patterns of behaviour. Furthermore, religious education is thought of as providing clear answers to questions about right and wrong and parents look for the development of positive moral views and codes of behaviour. For the majority of parents Christianity provides children with authoritative answers in terms of how they ought to behave.

Parents' replies are an indication of the importance they attach to religious education in church schools.

Having looked at the aims and content of religious education in both secondary and primary schools and having given consideration to expectations of parents it is now necessary to dwell on the variety of approaches adopted within the schools.

In twenty-one (55 per cent) church schools and sixteen (57 per cent) county schools RE teachers said they favoured an open-ended approach to religious education. These teachers saw their main task as one of enabling pupils to become aware of the relevance of a religious interpretation to life. Through knowledge, understanding, exploration and evaluation, it is hoped that the pupil would then be able to make an informed decision whether to accept and adopt a religious view to life. The essential difference between church and county school teachers' replies is that RE teachers in church schools were concerned primarily with enabling pupils to be informed about Christianity, the following abstract expresses this approach:

> My approach is one of enabling pupils to understand what it is to be a Christian in the full sense of the word so that they can decide whether they want to accept or reject Christianity.

This approach is described by the Schools Council as a 'neo-confessional' approach which it sees as an attempt '... to make "confessional" or dogmatic religious education more acceptable ...'. These attempts are usually liberal in intention, and at secondary level their approach is often described as 'open-ended'. However, this is an 'open-ended' approach to Christianity.'[16] Five county teachers also see their approach as an open-ended approach to Christianity.

The remaining eleven RE teachers in county schools who said they adopt an open-ended approach share the following view:-

> My approach is open-ended because I am teaching them about belief and promoting understanding. It is for them to question and weigh up things. Discussion plays an important part. It is a subject with no definitive proof and this leads to a lot of healthy discussion.

The replies in this group can be identified with the 'phenomenological' approach which the Schools Council sees '... as the promotion of understanding'. It uses the tools of scholarship in order to enter into empathic experience of the faith of individuals and groups. It does not seek to promote any one religious viewpoint but it recognizes that the study of religion must transcend the merely informative.[17]

Seven county (25 per cent) and three (8 per cent) church school teachers did not explicitly state that their approach was open-ended. Their answers implied they were not concerned with providing pupils with a religious interpretation to life. The approach was an objective examination of religion geared to their pupils acquiring knowledge and meeting exam requirements. The study of religion was an end in itself and not a means to some undetermined end. These replies fit the Schools Council's 'anti-dogmatic approach'. 'This [approach] rules out the subjective element from religious education and conceives it as an academic exercise, dispassionate and objective'.[18]

Fourteen (37 per cent) RE teachers in church schools and one RE teacher in a county school said their approach to RE was not open-ended. The county teacher described his approach in the following way 'certainly my approach is not open-ended. Our assumptions are that

Christianity is the true religion... We look at Christianity as a way of life. We look at the relationship of ourselves to God, thus we have to look at what being a Christian means.' Referring to the RE staff a church school teacher pointed out that 'The position of the staff teaching religious education is clear. They are not open-ended in their approach because they are all practitioners including myself.' The Schools Council describes this approach as the 'confessional' or dogmatic approach. 'This begins with the assumption that the aim of religious education is intellectual and cultic indoctrination. It is often linked with the belief that any other kind of religious education is unworthy of its name'.[19] It is doubtful if teachers in this group would see any other form of religious education as 'unworthy of its name'. However, for these RE teachers in church schools, if a descriptive or open-ended approach to religious education is adopted where the teacher is not explicitly teaching for commitment on the part of the pupils then religious education will not differ significantly from that provided in county schools. In which case, for these teachers, one justification for church schools would be called into question.

In an attempt to discover whether teachers thought religious education should be different in church and county schools RE teachers were asked whether religious education in church and county schools should differ in aims, content and approach. Replies to this question are given in the following table:

TABLE 36: RE teachers' views on whether religious education should differ in church and county schools in aims, content and approach

	Church	County
Aims		
Yes, should differ	22	15
No	15	10
Don't know	1	3
Content		
Yes, should differ	20	15
No	11	10
Don't know	17	3
Approach		
Yes, should differ	15	15
No	17	9
Don't know	6	4

Turning to look at the reasons why county school RE teachers thought that aims should be different, one teacher explains:

My experience of church schools is that they are different. Their aims are more to do with developing faith, belief and commitment to a particular religion and this is not the task of religious education in a secular school.

Other teachers mentioned there are more Christian children in church schools and they can, therefore, assume an understanding of, and in some cases, a commitment to Christianity whereas the same assumptions cannot be made in a county school. Far more is seen as possible in a church school in terms of 'Christian visual settings, church services, worship and Christian staff'. Teachers also referred to parents expectations of church schools — 'Parents expect catechesis'.

Teachers' replies which confirm that the aims should be the same fall into two distinct groups. First, five county teachers see their schools as providing Christian nurture. For one teacher his school is 'a Christian community just as much as the church school would be'. Second, the aim of religious education is to enable children to understand about religion and its relevance to life, and therefore, there should be no difference between church and county schools.

RE teachers in church schools who said the aims should be different shared the view that 'the aims must be different because the ethos is deliberately different'. 'Here the aim is to teach the faith and we don't hide it.' Other teachers pointed out that 'a county school has to place Christianity alongside other religions in an objective way whereas in church schools the aim is to study religion from the inside'.

The main reason given for a different content in religious education is that church schools devote far more time to the study of Christianity and a strong emphasis is placed on Anglican teaching. A county teacher expressed this view in the following way:

> In a church school there is an allegiance to a basic tradition. The content will differ and must differ. It would be wrong to include Anglican teaching in a county school. They would be more doctrinal, for example, on subjects like abortion and the church view would probably dominate. This is where we must differ...
> It's a dilemma for me as an RE teacher. Perhaps I should be more of a guiding influence than just giving facts.

Where teachers said the content should not differ they thought that all schools should be teaching world religions and responding to the fact of religious and cultural pluralism in society.

Turning to look at the reasons why approaches to religious education should differ, the dominant view expressed suggested that teachers in church schools are teaching for a commitment to Christianity, reinforcing or nurturing faith. County teachers also mentioned that church schools were involved in 'induction' and indoctrination into religion. A sizeable number of RE teachers in county schools see the approach adopted in the church schools as 'confessional' but not necessarily open-ended. For teachers in church schools their approach differs because they are approaching the study of Christianity from the inside as committed Christians.

The Swann Report shares the view expressed by the Schools Council that:

> The confessional aim, though perfectly proper with a community of faith, is not appropriate within schools serving a multi-belief society. Moreover, it conflicts at several points with the principles on which education is based. (p. 474)

It is firmly in favour of the 'phenomenological' approach to religious education which it sees '... as the best and indeed the only means of enhancing the understanding of all pupils, from whatever religious background, of the plurality of faiths in contemporary Britain, of bringing them to an understanding of the nature of belief and the religious dimension of human existence, and of helping them to appreciate the diverse and sometimes conflicting life stances which exist and thus enabling them to determine (and justify) their own religious position.' Furthermore, the Swann Report sees the phenomenological approach to religious education '... as the only response that accords with the fundamental principles underlying the ideal of cultural pluralism' (p. 475).

It can be argued that in setting goals for religious education the Swann Report, with its emphasis on the multicultural character of the contemporary classroom, gives primacy to cultural and social phenomena. The main focus is on society-centred preoccupations. The phenomenological approach which itself attempts to 'transcend the merely formative' seeks to 'elucidate' and at the same time establish a balance which does justice to the religious diversity in society.

The Swann Report is concerned primarily with a secular response to religious pluralism in society. Phillips makes a useful distinction between 'elucidation' and 'advocacy' and he points out that if religion is to be taught in schools then a distinction must be made between the two. He considers the former — elucidation — to be the appropriate method of teaching religion in schools.[20] The Swann Report is also taking the view that this is the only appropriate teaching method.

God's call to man provides the starting point for many church schools and their various activities within the schools — assemblies, Christian worship, Eucharistic services, denominational teaching, and religious education classes are all aimed at enabling the child to listen. At this point the stance of the church school becomes child-centred. The church school is, and indeed must also be involved in elucidation for as Brenda Watson succinctly puts it, '... the astonishing affirmations of Christianity invite denial or acceptance, neither of which can usefully be given without much thought and study; the adult who cannot give an intelligent response, from a position of some knowledge, can be accused of being superficial in his attitude towards life.'[21]

Church and county schools have both identified what they see as the aims of religious education which will be conducive to preparing pupils to live in a culturally and religiously diverse society. In general, we have seen that for the majority of county schools, and for a minority of church schools, the dominant feature of religious education is one of elucidation — teaching about religion. While on the other hand, for the majority of church schools and a minority of county schools, religious education is concerned with elucidation and advocacy — education into religion, where a major emphasis is placed on the Christian faith.

Governors of church schools are provided with the facility to appoint Christians to teach religious education. This feature provides the context where Christian nurture is offered by Christians 'in order to strengthen the Christian faith and develop Christian character',[22] an opportunity not guaranteed in county schools, although this is not to deny that Christian nurture is not the aim in some county schools.

While the majority of church schools take as their starting point the call of God, of primary concern is the Christian facility to hear that call. It does not preclude the possibility of a general opening of God's message transmitted through other faiths.

We have seen throughout this chapter that our multibelief society presents new challenges for all schools. There is an acknowledgement of one another's right to be different. This mutual acceptance reflects a major change in religious education and RE teachers in many schools have not yet equipped themselves fully to cope with this change.

Church schools have the potential to develop a different approach to the study of world religions from that of county schools. In addition to elucidation they can, as the British Council of Churches point out, 'aim for the open-hearted dialogue in faith, an encounter of religions which enriches faith, for the conversation between religions is from the inside.'[23] To the believer, the view from within is vital for a real understanding of his religion. Here then, is an important challenge to church schools — how to communicate the Christian faith within a multifaith classroom, and maintain the integrity of mainstream Christian endeavour, while at the same time respecting the faiths of all pupils in

Religious Education

such a way that they are not tolerated extras nor are they merely studied purely to avoid 'unintentional rudeness', but that they are accepted for what they are — living religions which are flourishing in a shared environment. Clearly such a goal cannot be achieved in schools where religious education is given a low status or where RE teachers do not have the confidence or the expertise to teach world religions.

While some church schools no longer accept that religious education in the classroom should be concerned with Christian nurture, the majority of church schools demonstrate that in potential, education and nurture can exist harmoniously side by side. For some RE teachers Christian nurture is not seen as restrictive nor does it involve foreclosing rational options. The British Council of Churches, in their detailed analysis of Christian nurture, point out that if Christian nurture is to exist alongside secular education 'critical openness' must be seen as central to nurture. Furthermore, they state, 'secular education and Christian nurture share the same spirit of critical openness'. They illustrate how critical openness and autonomy, while similar, are not identical. Both are concerned with the individual thinking for himself in a reasoned way and both imply a process of growth, but they have differing goals. Christian nurture seeks to 'deepen the Christian faith and life', while secular education is compatible with a wide range of religious and non-religious philosophies. The British Council of Churches, however, make a very important distinction between autonomy and critical openness when they point out that:

> To be open is to listen to be ready to receive other persons, to hear new ideas, to re-examine one's own past, whereas autonomy could perhaps suggest a certain isolation, even a self-enclosed independence, or it might suggest individualism, whereas critical openness is intended to suggest one is in a community, a learning community, in which one speaks and listens, being both critical and receptive. A pre-requisite of learning is humility. You must recognise that there is something to be learned and that it is worth learning. The term 'critical openness' suggests better than the term 'autonomy' this humility and this probing towards the unknown.[24]

The British Council of Churches point out that 'the witness of the Christian schools must be robust'. For:

> Not only will the Christian nurture they offer to their pupils be nobler, but the service rendered to the secular schools will also be enhanced. Of course, there is no value in merely being an

alternative to the state school system. But let there be schools which in their teaching and structures explicitly and implicitly allow the light of the Christian gospel to search the value assumptions of contemporary life and education, and they will tend to become a valuable alternative. They will constitute a challenge to the state schools which naturally reflect the wider values of modern thought and life ...[25]

Additional Replies of RE Teachers Relating to the Teaching of World Religions

Q.18. Are religions other than Christianity dealt with in RE classes? If so, does the choice of religions studied reflect the faiths of pupils?

Yes   No

'No, we choose Islam, Judaism and Christianity because we think they can be successfully taught. I have taught Hinduism and Buddhism but I have found that this confuses the children. They are too profound. Their philosophy should be left until the sixth form when the children can understand them.' (Church)

'No. The choice wasn't done for that reason, but we do have a few Muslims in the school and also a very few Hindus. I chose Judaism because you need an understanding of this for understanding Christianity and to see the links. I chose Islam because it is a world phenomenon and they will come into contact with Muslims. Hinduism was chosen because it is so different, although it is very difficult to understand. It has so many aspects in it that are religious.' (Church)

'This tends to overlap into issues of multi-faith problems. For example, the Koran is a document which is not to be criticized. Muslims cannot accept that it is symbolic or that it is a story, therefore, we have to be careful. We have to treat it differently from other texts. This is just an example of the problems we encounter in teaching about other faiths.' (Church)

'In the lower school we look at Christianity, Hinduism, Islam and Judaism. The choice of religions studied does not reflect the faiths of pupils. I chose Judaism for the first year because it is more straightforward. Islam in the second year and Hinduism in the third year. Hinduism is more difficult to get close to. I chose three religions

Religious Education

because we wanted one for each year and they are also the major world religions and the ones that teachers feel more confident in teaching rather than Buddhism or other non-religious world views.' (County)

'No, because the school is mostly a group of Christians. We do Hinduism, Judaism, Mohammedism and Sikhism. The reason for choosing these are that they are the principle religions of the world. In fact world religions is not really my subject, however, I will be teaching it in the fourth year.' (Church)

'The religions chosen are those that we feel that we can do well. I am not into the Cooks Tour business. I would rather do fewer world religions and do them thoroughly.' (Church)

'Not really, because there are very few pupils with other religions in the school. She said that she chose Islam because it is related to the Jewish/Christian faith, also two out of three of the RE members of staff know something about Islam — one has lived in Iran.' (Church)

Q.24. Is it possible for RE in your school to do justice to the different religious backgrounds of pupils?

Yes   No

'No. The problems are firstly the amount of staffing. This is not adequate, although you get enthusiastic help from people. This is not a substitute for the type of interest and commitment from specialists who want to deepen their knowledge. Secondly, it also shows in the curriculum. It is extraordinary to provide the D Form children with RE rather than the A Form where there is the notion that they need to concentrate on more sophisticated subjects. Thirdly, the idea that there is no RE in the fourth and fifth years unless they do the 'O' level or the CSE as well. They are just becoming aware of others at this stage and what it is like to relate to others.' (County)

Q.25. Do you think that children of different faiths should be taught by teachers professing the same faith?

Yes   No

Faith, Culture and the Dual System

'No I think it takes us back to the turn of the century. There it led to bigotry and producing a stable society in the wrong kind of way with no fluidity or movement in it. One wonders whether there is any openness in a procedure which may be more instruction rather than education i.e., it might be akin to Sunday Schools.' (County)

'No. Do we mean faiths here or denominations? In a church school we would not appoint a Sikh or a Muslim to teach RE because of the nature of the school. I would expect the RE staff in a church school to have a faith. Whether that is a strong faith or a search for faith is immaterial.' (Church)

'No. If you are going to pretend to teach them their faith then yes, but they don't want that and wouldn't come here if they did. We teach what the majority want, i.e., core Christianity and teach other religions in that setting.' (Church)

'No, one thing I am conscious of in being Christian is that it is a narrow outlook to look at other religions from. Conversely, there is a problem that you cannot be expert in all religions at the same time.' (Church)

'Not at this school. Policy of school not to offer an alternative. Parents know the school rules when they apply for a place for their child.' (Church)

'As an RE teacher I do not feel I can do justice to other faiths and nurture children in their non-Christian faiths.' (Church)

It might be more difficult though to get inside a faith system if you don't have one yourself.' (Church)

'No, not in a church school. Those of other faiths send their children to this school with the knowledge that we are a Church of England school and we have not had complaints that we are not teaching Islam, etc.' (Church)

'No, this would be impractical, but also as far as one teaches about the world religions one can do that just as easily as say talking about different trees in the world. You don't have to be committed to them to talk about them. I think of my teaching aims to be descriptive of things and it should be possible to be objective about what we are describing.' (County)

'No, not necessarily, unless the teacher is particularly bigotted and does not want to embrace anything.' (County)

'As a Christian I could teach Islam, but possibly not very well. He or she wouldn't perhaps have the necessary commitment for it to come across. He said that this was one of the biggest questions in religious studies at the moment. However, he was confident to say that I believe it is important that teachers of religion do have an experience of a religion at least.' (County)

'No, it is impractical. This is not possible in a State school. In this sort of school we have few children apart from the main stream Christians, even in a multi-racial school it might not be possible. If people of another faith come to this country, the children are going to have to grow up in a Christian society and should learn about it.' (County)

'Yes, ideally, just as I believe RE and Christianity should be done by people who are Christians. This viewpoint is partly from a purely practical point of view, I do not think that any one can be expected to be reasonably competent in a number of religions, also I do not think the Western mind can grasp some of the philosophical ideas of the Eastern religions despite what might have been said.' (County)

Notes

1 NATIONAL SOCIETY (1972) *The Fourth R*, The Durham Report on Religious Education, second edition, London, SPCK, p. 103.
2 WATSON, B. *Education, Life and Christian Belief*, Oxford, The Farmington Institute for Christian Studies, p. 37.
3 SMART, N. and HORDER, N. (1975) 'Editors Preface', in SMART, N. and HORDER, D. (Eds.) *New Movements in Religious Education*. London, Temple Smith.
4 COLE, W.O. (1983) *Religion in the Multi-faith School*, London, Hutton, p. 11.
5 SCHOOLS COUNCIL (1971) *Religious Education in Secondary Schools*, Working Party 36, Evans/ Methuen Educational for the Schools Council, p. 15.
6 DURKHEIM, E. (1956) *Education and Sociology*, Glencoe, Ill.
7 COLE, W.O. (1982) 'Religion in the multi-faith school', in HULL, J. *New Directions in Religious Education*, Lewes, Falmer Press, p. 174.
8 GERLOFF, R. (1984) *The Development of Black Churches in Britain since 1952*, paper presented to the conference on The Development and Impact

of New Religious Movements, King's College, London, p. 9.
9 RODGER, A.R. (1982) *Education and Faith in an Open Society*, Handsel Press, p. 114.
10 SCHOOLS COUNCIL (1971) *op. cit.*, p. 66.
11 HULL, J. (1984) *Studies in Religion and Education*, Lewes, Falmer Press, pp. 53 and 81.
12 *15 to 18: A Report of the Central Advisory Council for Education (England)* (1959) Volume 1, London, HMSO.
13 RODGER, A. (1982) *op. cit.*, p. 125.
14 Department of Education and Science (1967) *Children and their Primary Schools: A Report of the Central Advisory Council for Education (England)*, Vol. 1, London, HMSO, p. 207, para. 572.
15 NATIONAL SOCIETY (1972), *op. cit.*, p. 251.
16 SCHOOLS COUNCIL (1971) *op. cit.*, p. 30.
17 *Ibid.* p. 21.
18 *Ibid.*
19 *Ibid.*
20 PHILIPS, D.Z. (1970) 'Philosophy and religious education', *British Journal of Educational Studies*, XVLLL, 1, pp. 13–14.
21 WATSON, B. *op. cit.*, p. 41.
22 BRITISH COUNCIL OF CHURCHES (1981) *Understanding Christian Nurture*, British Council of Churches, p. 99.
23 *Ibid.* p. 99.
24 *Ibid.* p. 7.
25 *Ibid.* p. 100.

Chapter 7

Multicultural Education

In order to understand what is happening in schools in their response to multicultural education it is necessary to outline briefly those educational principles, practices and policies which have come to be collectively known as multicultural education.

In the early 1950s it was recognized that the arrival of large numbers of immigrants from new commonwealth countries had far-reaching implications for schools. Britain was then generally perceived as a relatively homogenous culture and the initial response of the education system was one of absorbing immigrant children into mainstream education with as little disruption as possible to the education of the indigenous children. The major task for schools was seen as making provision for teaching English as a second language to provide for the needs of immigrant children.

Concern was often expressed, particularly by indigenous parents, that their children's education would be adversely affected in schools with predominantly immigrant rolls. These fears were noted by the government of the day which responded to the new situation with a policy which included dispersal of children:

> It is inevitable that, as the proportion of immigrant children in a school increases, the problems will be more difficult to solve, and the chances of assimilation more remote. How far any given proportion of immigrant children can be absorbed with benefit to both sides depends on, among other factors, the number of immigrant children who are proficient in English; the dividing line cannot be precisely defined. Experience suggests, however, that ... up to a fifth of immigrant children in any group fit in with reasonable ease, but that, if the proportion goes over about one-third either in the school as a whole or in any one class, serious strains arise. It is therefore desirable that the catchment

areas of schools should, wherever possible, be arranged to avoid undue concentrations of immigrant children. Where this proves impracticable ... every effort should be made to disperse the immigrant children round a greater number of schools ...[1]

The assimilationist approach adopted was thus characterized by a response that featured the educational needs of, and the language provision for, immigrant children to be accompanied by a policy of dispersal. The underlying assumption was that immigrant children must adapt to British society. There was no acknowledgement of the importance for these children to retain their cultural and religious lifestyles.

The assimilationist approach failed to achieve the specified objectives. The 'problems' of immigrants did not disappear as was anticipated. Their cultural identities did not simply dissolve nor were they subsumed within the majority culture.

In the light of the failure of the assimilationist approach a new integrationist model was devised. This approach still focussed on the need to assimilate ethnic minority groups but at the same time it recognized the validity of different life-styles, cultural and religious backgrounds. There was a move away from mutual superiority to mutual tolerance. In 1966 Roy Jenkins as Home Secretary defined integration '... not as a flattening process of assimilation but as equal opportunity accompanied by cultural diversity in an atmosphere of mutual tolerance'.

By the end of the 1960s and early 1970s there was a growing awareness that the policies and practices adopted by proponents of the integrationist approach had not achieved the desired results. Immigrant pupils were seen to have educational needs which schools had failed to come to terms with. One indicator of this failure was the underachievement of West Indian pupils.[2]

A shift then followed away from the integrationist approach to a perspective that emphasized cultural diversity. The main stress was on the importance of teaching about the cultures of ethnic minority pupils both as a means of developing a 'positive self-image' among black pupils and of providing for white pupils a greater appreciation and awareness of cultural diversity:

As the Swann Committee points out:

> The most obvious difference between the early days of assimilation and integration, and the concept of multicultural education is that whereby the former focussed primarily on seeking to 'remedy' the perceived 'problems' of ethnic minority

children and to 'compensate' for their perceived 'disabilities', multicultural education has usually tended to have two distinct themes — firstly, meeting the particular educational needs of ethnic minority children and secondly, the broader issue of preparing all pupils for life in a multi-racial society. (p. 199)

Today, there is a growing recognition, however, that a cultural pluralism approach, while attempting to promote mutual respect and understanding between cultural groups, fails to come to terms with racism in all its forms. The Inner London Education Authority, for example, while recognizing the positive aspects of a perspective which emphasizes cultural diversity believes that this approach ignores or denies racism and the need to promote racial equality; also differential access to resources, and the power relations between white and black people are not catered for. For the Inner London Education Authority a perspective emphasizing equality is a crucial starting point. [ILEA] 'is committed to achieving equality in education... This means the development of an education service from which racism, sexism and class discrimination and prejudice have been eliminated so that the Authority can respond fully to the needs of our multiethnic society'.[3]

The view that multicultural education has relevance for all children was given recognition in the 1977 Government Green Paper *Education in Schools: A Consultative Document*, which states that 'our society is a multicultural, multiracial one and the curriculum should reflect a sympathetic understanding of the different cultures and races that now make up our society ... the curriculum of schools must reflect the needs of this new Britain'.[4] Also in 1977, the General Synod affirmed the multicultural and multiracial nature of our society and called for 'an appropriate educational programme'.[5] Multicultural education became the path educationalists and policy makers followed in shaping an appropriate educational programme for a multicultural society.

In 1983, six years after the General Synod advocated an appropriate educational programme for what they described as a multicultural and multiracial society, the General Synod Board of Education issued a discussion paper on multicultural education. It was intended as a basis for discussion and therefore did not set out to provide multicultural initiatives or provide answers for teachers in church schools. At a national level this discussion document remains the major contribution to the vital and challenging debate concerning multicultural education[6] made by the Church of England.

At a local level, five out of nine Diocesan Boards of Education in our study have developed multicultural education initiatives for their schools. In addition, they have organized seminars and conferences to enable teachers to discuss and work out their objectives regarding multicultural education. The Southwark Diocesan Board of Education has also established a multiethnic working party.

Ten out of fourteen local education authorities have formulated policies on multicultural education. Eight of these authorities have appointed a multicultural inspector or adviser. In addition, nine authorities have provided multicultural resource centres.

Although the concept of multicultural education is widely used there are, however, many varying interpretations and definitions. Accordingly, no agreed consensus exists in the education world as to what constitutes multicultural education. The term is used to cover a range of different practices such as developing self-image, teaching of mother tongue language, bilingual competence, dietary needs, racial discrimination and a critique of racism and ethnocentrism. Mal Philips-Bell has identified three main ways in which the term is used. However, these different uses are not necessarily exclusive.[7] First, 'education through many cultures' whereby teachers draw upon the diverse elements issuing from different cultures. 'Education is brought about through the use of these elements in teaching'. The extent to which cultural diversity is reflected in teaching will depend upon, as Philips-Bell points out, the particular conception of education involved and 'whether these multicultural elements are regarded as logically, psychologically or morally necessary, or as not necessary but optional'. Second, multicultural education when used to refer to 'education into many cultures', is based on the underlying assumption that to understand and gain insight into other cultures 'is worthwhile, either in itself or as a means to good "race relations" '. Third, multicultural education meaning 'education for a multicultural society': As Philips-Bell points out 'it is a wider conception than the previous two insofar as many more practical implications follow. It implies a determination to work towards bringing about social change both in schools and society by eliminating institutional racism and promoting equality and justice'.

With the first two conceptions of multicultural education the focus is on cultural diversity and the main implication for teachers is that they must be knowledgeable about different cultural groups. But with the third conception, many 'race' and 'education' issues are involved. Issues include the development of self-image and negative racial attitudes, the racial bias in books and materials and teacher attitudes and expectations.[8]

However, critics of multicultural education have argued that it is a means of 'containing the black problem' and it fails to come to terms with racism. Farrukh Dhondy dismisses multicultural education and refers to

Multicultural Education

it as '... a massive public relations exercise ... that the Schools Council, the Humanities Curriculum Project and other white-haired respectables have disseminated as an answer to the contradictions that black youth point up in the schools.'[9]

Recognizing the complexity of the concept of multicultural education, it was important to explore what was actually happening in schools. Headteachers were asked a number of open-ended questions enabling them to express in their own way what they perceived to be the aims and purposes of multicultural education (table 37) and how they interpreted or measured progress in this whole area.

TABLE 37: Secondary headteachers' replies to the question — what in your view are the aims and purposes of multicultural education?

	Church	County
	(percentage in brackets)	
Prepare pupils for a multicultural society	12 (32)	11 (39)
Provide for the needs of ethnic minority groups	12 (32)	7 (25)
Integration	6 (16)	—
Ensure no unfair discrimination	5 (13)	5 (18)
A questioning of Anglo-Saxon values	—	1 (3.5)
Never thought about it. Don't know	8 (21)	6 (21)
Combating racism	3 (8)	6 (21)

Note: Eight headteachers in church schools and eight teachers in county schools stated more than one aim.

A number of observations can be made concerning headteachers' replies on the aims and purposes of multicultural education. First, a majority of all headteachers have emphasized the needs of ethnic minority groups. Second, just under a quarter of church and county schools have not formulated any views on the aims and purposes of multicultural education.

Four of the church school headteachers who saw multicultural education mainly in terms of the integration of ethnic minority groups were expressing their views in relation to other schools with ethnic minority pupil composition. As their own schools are situated in 'white' suburban areas multicultural education was seen as irrelevant within their social contexts. In their replies these teachers spoke of 'a more comfortable integration of the various strands of society'; 'we must always be thinking of integration into society' and 'integration is vital if we are going to have peaceful co-existence'. One headteacher qualified his view of multicultural education in the following way:

> It depends on what you call multicultural education. I believe that in the present context it should refer to our European

connection. The aim in this school through the teaching of French, German, Spanish and European studies is to bring children of the Common Market countries into a closer relationship by the use of all the languages spoken.

If multicultural education means Asian/West Indian awareness, it is a non-starter. When a person emigrates he/she should adopt the customs and attitudes of the host country. This is not an arrogant statement, it is common sense.

It is noteworthy that headteachers in the matching county schools to those church schools just mentioned shared the same integrationist view. Furthermore, two of the local education authorities in which three of these church schools are situated, have not yet developed any multicultural policies. While LEA initiatives are very important in determining policies and practices in many schools it is important to say, however, that the formulation of multicultural initiatives does not guarantee that all schools will reflect these initiatives. Evidence was available showing that many schools ignore such leads.

Headteachers who see multicultural education in terms of providing for the needs of ethnic minority groups take their educational needs as their starting point and consequently multicultural education is seen as having relevance for only a section of the school population.

The need to combat racism in schools and in society was explicitly mentioned by 8 per cent of church school headteachers and by just under a quarter of headteachers in county schools. However, it will be seen later that the need to counter racism was an important priority for more schools than would appear from these figures.

Twelve headteachers (32 per cent) in church schools and eleven (39 per cent) headteachers in county schools see multicultural education as preparing all pupils to take their place in a culturally diverse society.

Headteachers in secondary schools were also asked to give details concerning the progress (table 38) that had been made in developing multicultural education and to provide details of any curriculum changes.

The figures in table 38 show that church schools lag behind county schools in their perception of progress in developing multicultural education. Before turning to look at how headteachers measure this progress another observation needs to be made. While 79 per cent of headteachers in both church and county schools held clear views on the aims and purposes of multicultural education it does not necessarily follow that these views will always be translated into policies and practices in schools.

Headteachers who said they have made tremendous progress have

Multicultural Education

TABLE 38: Details of progress in developing multicultural education in secondary schools

	Church	County
	(percentage in brackets)	
Tremendous progress	–	7 (25)
Good progress		
Positive approach	9 (24)	3 (11)
Very limited progress	6 (16)	3 (11)
Working party established to look at issues involved	10 [26]	7 (25)
No progress	13 (34)	8 (28)

developed 'whole school strategies' in developing multicultural education. The following extract illustrates the approach adopted by these headteachers:

> Tremendous progress has been made. We have had a curriculum review. We are looking at all books and looking at what is displayed on the walls. We are emphasizing mother-tongue languages. There has been a basic questioning of values implicit in Anglo-Saxon values. This overhaul has been going on for about eighteen months... We have a black governor and four black members on the PTA. We also have five teachers of West Indian or Asian origin. This was a very positive move.

In this school a teacher had been appointed solely for the purpose of developing multiethnic education. This teacher is a Ugandan Asian and the headteacher observed that if West Indian children get into trouble or have problems they will ask for him to be present when they have to discuss their problems with the headteacher.

Another teacher in discussing the importance of visible displays of cultural diversity said that many children from ethnic minority groups have either experienced discrimination or 'feel invisible'. The use of 'multi-lingual signs around the school is seen as a way of showing pupils that their cultural background is positively valued in the school. In this school a working party had been established for over five years and it had arranged numerous conferences. The progress of the working party was outlined in the following way:

> They tackled racism first, particularly overt racism in the school. They asked me to participate in the social education class for two or three weeks when there was a National Front activity in the school. Every department has been asked to review their course content and resources to check for racism. Also to look for positive opportunities. After this the working party spread to look at the curriculum in all subject areas. A check list was produced for the benefit of each department.

Faith, Culture and the Dual System

These headteachers' replies convey the view that multicultural education must permeate the official curriculum as well as the hidden curriculum. To be meaningful it has to be as one headteacher put it, 'the very fibre of the place'. The emphasis is on understanding the differences and similarities of the diverse cultural groups which go to form a pluralistic society. The school ethos is one that fosters an appreciation of differences rather than striving to homogenize all cultural groups.

The progress made in these County schools is very much in line with the views expressed in the Swann Report on multicultural education. 'The Committee does not believe that education should seek to iron out the differences between cultures and not attempt to draw everyone into the dominant culture but rather should draw upon the experiences of the many cultures that make up our society and thus broaden the cultural horizons of every child' (p. 324).

Headteachers who said they had made good progress in developing multicultural education represent just under a quarter of county schools and 11 per cent of church secondary schools. For these headteachers a positive approach has been adopted in developing and implementing multicultural education and all teachers have been asked to review their subject areas. In these schools changes have occurred in at least two subject areas. Geography, history, religious education and, to a lesser extent, English, appear to be popular subjects for revision.

The category 'limited progress' includes statistics for schools where headteachers said that change had occurred in one subject only and seen as either appropriate or sufficient in developing multicultural education. More often than not, change was a result of the initiative of individual teachers. Development tended to be fragmented. The following extracts illustrate this point:

> I touch upon it [multicultural education] in the design for living course which I teach but this is only part of a couple of lessons in the course of a whole year. We do look at prejudice, I think, in the RE course, but this will be up to the RE teacher.

Another said:

> A lot goes on in the RE department. I haven't really noticed progress elsewhere, perhaps in the world studies course in geography, but I am not sure.

We have seen in the previous chapter that there is room for improvement in what is happening in religious education classes in some schools, in terms of providing accurate information in a competent and confident way. Many teachers give it a low status, offer it as an

Multicultural Education

optional subject and yet so much is expected from religious education.

In ten (26 per cent) church schools and seven (25 per cent) county schools working parties have been established to enable the schools to identify the issues involved, produce a statement on multicultural education and to look at the procedures for implementing curriculum change.

In thirteen church and eight county schools according to headteachers' comments no progress had been made in developing multicultural education. Three distinct reasons were given. The following two extracts, the first from a headteacher in a county school and the second from a church school headteacher, illustrate the approach that takes as its starting point 'We treat them all the same', which is often referred to as the 'colour blind' approach:

> I can only answer by saying I have the responsibility here for 560 children regardless of race or religion. I treat them all as equals and hopefully afford equal opportunity for all. I therefore like to think that the word 'multicultural education' has zero relevance here.

> Progress is a loaded word. There is an awful lot of fantasy going on in schools regarding multicultural education. We would regard our treatment of Africans and other ethnic groups as inherently fair and equal. Just because they were oppressed years ago we will not give them special treatment now, but we will help them with teaching difficulties or other educational difficulties. There are plenty of secular schools they can opt for. Look at the essence of Christianity — this is a communion of people — our head boy is in fact a coloured boy.

At the core of this headteacher's reply is a 'problem-centred' perspective which perceives multicultural education as having only one dimension relating to the needs of ethnic minority groups.

The second view expressed also emphasizes the needs of ethnic minority groups but in addition multicultural education is perceived as relevant only to schools where pupils' backgrounds are culturally diverse:

> Why get involved when it does not affect you. Here they are mainly one generation English... If half my pupils were from Pakistan then I would have to have some Pakistani staff to teach them about their culture if this is what they wanted. My experience is that most want to be treated as English.

Faith, Culture and the Dual System

A third view expressed suggested that multicultural education can be harmful and divisive and that 'children don't like people talking to them about preserving their black culture anyway — it remains a dubious one'. Another teacher in a church school in discussing the reasons why the school had not developed multicultural education made the following observation:

> No progress has been made in the sense that we do anything specifically designed to cater for different racial groups. I have never taught in a multicultural school. There is a gap in my experience. This is the situation of most of my staff. The concept of multicultural education has got itself into a ghetto-like situation. There has developed a ghetto-like pattern of thought. The children live well together. It's the adults who cause the problems. For example, when a Muslim mum says that she won't let her girl do so and so, it sets up barriers. We don't have many coloured children here, it is between thirty and forty. I have never been aware and my colleagues don't seem to be aware that they have felt, or been made to feel, any different. Most of the problems are with the adults.

Clearly in these extracts it is easy to discern the preoccupation with one of the fundamental principles of the assimilationist philosophy — ethnic provision without affecting the majority of pupils.

Finally a minority of headteachers dismissed multicultural education as trendy, the 'in-thing' or as one headteacher put it — 'Frankly, I have the feeling this is a bandwagon and I don't particularly approve'.

In 60 per cent of church secondary schools and 53 per cent of county schools, the school ethos, curriculum, policies and practices remain unchanged by the cultural diversity to be found outside the school environment. Even in the presence of cultural diversity within the school many remained unaffected. On a number of occasions headteachers in church schools remarked that the pupils are 'all Christians' — consequently no change was envisaged despite the fact that pupils of West Indian origin constitute a considerable percentage of the pupil population. As a result of seeing multicultural education in relation to the school environment only, these schools have adopted an inward-looking philosophy. They have yet to acknowledge or be convinced of the need to evaluate the school's aims and objectives in the light of a changed society.

Considering the varying interpretations among theorists it is not surprising that the same lack of universal acceptance or consensus on the aims and purposes of multicultural education is present among

Multicultural Education

headteachers. The anomalies and inconsistencies concerning headteachers' views in the area of multicultural education reflect the wider contradictions that are apparent within the social structure of modern Britain. While government policy-makers, educationalists, theorists and teachers may all be committed to the same basic values of justice, equality and tolerance, there appears to be very little consensus on programmes of action to achieve these goals.

Although the debate on multicultural education has shifted from a perspective emphasizing cultural diversity to an emphasis on challenging racism which involves combating prejudice resulting from ignorance, countering inaccurate stereotypes and the range of myths that exist about ethnic minority groups there was little evidence to show of this shift in schools. The point needs to be made that with a framework of anti-racist education there are a range of positions and perspectives adopted.

The Rampton Report defined racism in the following way:

> In our view racism describes a set of attitudes and behaviour towards people of another race which is based on the belief that races are distinct and can be graded as 'superior or inferior'. A racist is therefore someone who believes that people of a particular race, colour or national origin are inherently inferior, so that their identity, culture, self-esteem, views and feelings are of less value than his or her own and can be disregarded or treated as less important.[10]

Eleven headteachers (39 per cent) of county schools and five (13 per cent) church school headteachers said that multicultural education includes teaching to enable pupils to become aware of racial discrimination, bias, stereotyping, racial myths and the damage they cause. It was evident from our discussions with headteachers that the majority had not considered the possibility of including these areas for study. In one church school, their inclusion was dismissed for the following reasons:

> I believe it is foolish to do so. In my own view and I have a wide Jewish background, I am certain that positive discrimination has done more harm to the cause of total integration than any other single factor with the exception of the Race Relations Board. I think it is unfortunate that the Church of England has jumped on the bandwagon without really understanding the nature of the problems involved.

Where these areas are included in the curriculum they are usually covered in living and growing courses and social and general studies.

Faith, Culture and the Dual System

The majority of schools which include issues of racism in the curriculum are situated in inner London which suggests that the Inner London Education Authority's strong policy lead is having an effect in county schools, although to date its effect in church schools remains minimal.

The Swann Report gives education an important role in eliminating racism which it sees as a major obstacle to creating a truly pluralist society. It asserts that schools must be committed to equality and justice and a crucial element in developing the aim of 'Education for All' is the need to identify the practices or procedures which operate 'directly or indirectly, intentionally or unintentionally against pupils from any ethnic group'.

> Much of the task in countering and overcoming racism is concerned with attitude change and with encouraging youngsters to develop positive attitudes towards the multi-racial nature of society, free from the influence of inaccurate myths and stereotypes about other ethnic groups. (p. 321)

The Swann Report believes that this approach is essential in 'all white' schools. From the statistics collected it can be seen that there is very little progress being made in this area in either 'all white schools' or in schools with multicultural rolls. Indeed, many teachers are convinced that the best way to deal with racist matters is on an individual level. This type of response has the effect of seeing racist behaviour in isolation — a snap shot approach is adopted — deal with it and then forget about it — rather than looking for the underlying causes or attitudes which promote unacceptable behaviour. For the Swann Report this approach is unacceptable. 'We believe that for schools to allow racist attitudes to persist unchecked in fact constitutes a fundamental mis-education for their pupils.' (p. 36)

On more than one occasion a neutral approach could be detected in some of the comments made on racist behaviour. An RE teacher in a church school in responding to a question on the teaching of world religions demonstrates this point:

> I can't really comment because of the few other faiths in the school. Some of our children here are racist. I happened to have heard one of the two Hindus in the fifth form discussion group defending her right to be here. The view amongst the majority of the children is that immigrants should go home. Only having two Hindus in the school can be embarassingly difficult. If you had half a dozen in a discussion group of eighteen or so, then it

Multicultural Education

would be all right, but if you only have two then it can become very personal.

The need for care and compassion within the school is highlighted by this teacher who was apparently unaware that the Hindu girls in their isolation were very vulnerable and the situation called for more than mere embarrassment on the part of the teacher. In addition, the view expressed of safety in numbers misread a situation which called for a firm stand by the school to enable pupils to realize that their comments were distressing, damaging and inaccurate and that the school has an important role to play in countering racist behaviour.

Four major reports have been published since 1980 which focus on the education of black children today.[11] The Rampton Report, in confirming that West Indian children are being disadvantaged in the educational system, sees racism in schools as a contributory factor in their under-achievement:

> We are convinced from the evidence that we have obtained that racism both intentional and unintentional, has a direct and important bearing on the performance of West Indian children in our schools.[12]

The Rampton Committee found evidence of a wide range of myths and stereotypes of different ethnic groups and points to a lack of knowledge and understanding as an important factor in the growth and distribution of racial prejudice. Despite all that has been written on this subject the majority of headteachers in this study have either failed to see or dismissed the need to evaluate their school's policies and practices and their own attitudes. In discussing racism in schools and the ways in which schools can be oblivious to the impact of racism the Swann Report states:

> If in the face of such forms of racism, or indeed in the face of ignorance and inaccurate statements about ethnic minorities, the school seeks simply to remain neutral and uninvolved we would see this not only as a failure in terms of educational responsibilities but also as in effect condoning and thereby encouraging the persistence of such occurrences. Certainly it is difficult for ethnic minority communities to have full confidence and trust in institutions which they see as simply ignoring or dismissing what is in fact an ever present and all pervasive shadow over their everyday lives. (p. 35)

Faith, Culture and the Dual System

The General Synod of the Church of England Board of Education in its discussion paper on multicultural education fails to consider racism within the context of the evidence provided in the Rampton Report. In an unpublished article Kenneth Leech of the Board for Social Responsibility draws attention to this serious omission.[13] It is not possible to do justice to the concept of multicultural education while ignoring the social phenomenon of racism which is well documented in the major reports published in recent years.

In seventeen (61 per cent) county schools, one or more teachers had a specific responsibility for multicultural education. In sixteen (57 per cent) schools, teachers have attended conferences, courses or seminars. In addition, in eight (29 per cent) of these schools, teachers have received in-service training on developing and implementing a multicultural curriculum.

Turning to look at church schools we found only ten (26 per cent) schools where one or more teachers have a specific responsibility for multicultural education. In fourteen (37 per cent) schools teachers have attended conferences, courses or seminars and in seven (18 per cent) schools teachers had received in-service training.

When the statistics were analyzed to ascertain responsibility for multicultural education and whether they had received in-service training or attended courses or conferences it became evident that a higher percentage of teachers in county schools not only had a direct responsibility for multicultural education, but more had received in-service training and attended courses than was the case in church schools.

Nine (32 per cent) county schools and twenty-two (58 per cent) church schools, did not have any teachers responsible for multicultural education, none of the teachers in these schools had received in-service training nor had they attended any conferences or courses in this area.

School activity in each of these three areas is far more pronounced in inner London schools and schools in the West Midlands. All three local education authorities concerned have developed multicultural education policies, each a resource centre with a multicultural/multi-ethnic adviser. This statement must be qualified in the case of church schools. Their relationship with LEA initiatives and positive progress in developing multicultural education is very variable. It is necessary to take individual diocesan initiatives into account.

In five outer London boroughs where the local education authorities have not formulated any policies on multicultural education, none of the county or church schools visited is involved in any of the activities described above.

Multicultural Education

These findings demonstrate that a strong correlation exists between local education authority initiatives, policies and the overall commitment to multicultural education and the positive progress and commitment of headteachers and staff in the field of multicultural education, backed in the case of church schools by Diocesan board support.

To sum up at this point, the greatest progress in developing multicultural education has taken place in county schools. Over one quarter of the county schools in the sample reported tremendous progress, whereas no headteachers in church schools made this claim. Sixty per cent of church schools had not made any changes to the curriculum although in just under half these schools working parties have been established to look at the issues involved in implementing multicultural education. The percentage of county schools in this group is lower — 53 per cent.

Primary school headteachers were asked to provide details of the ways in which different cultures and faiths are expressed in their schools. Seventeen (46 per cent) said that different faiths and cultures were not expressed. For the majority of these headteachers the question was seen as irrelevant because 'they don't exist in the school.' This view was expressed in the following way:

> We haven't really got any because of our intake. I don't see I can claim to have done anything in particular. Again, because we have so few children from ethnic minority groups. Not having many of them it is not really so relevant.

One headteacher said as it was a Church of England school it was not appropriate to express different faiths and cultures, while another two explained that different cultures and faiths were respected but not expressed. 'They are not overtly expressed but they are respected and not minimized or dismissed. In a Church of England school they [other faiths and cultures] should not be expressed.' Teachers in this group also expressed the view that we treat them all the same.

For a further three headteachers the emphasis is on integration — 'We have a few of these children from other countries and we stress integration and we start where the children are now. This usually involves help with the English language'. Teachers comments highlight another aspect — 'I don't really believe in highlighting differences. We all have to live together in the same country. If you highlight differences this makes integration all the more difficult.' The philosophy in these schools, also apparent in the third school, is one of assimilation, where the emphasis is on absorbing the pupils into the educational system and helping them to 'fit in'. Little or no attention has been given to the racial

Faith, Culture and the Dual System

and cultural differences that exist. Indeed cultural identity is ignored in the school environment. While there is very little to choose between the assimilationist and integrationist perspectives the latter does try to make allowances for the recognition of differences in the religious and cultural backgrounds of different groups. Both approaches are seen in retrospect by the Swann Committee as 'misguided and ill-founded' (p. 198).

Headteachers who were concerned to give expression to different faiths and cultures represent just over half (54 per cent) of the primary school sample. The most popular way of expressing diversity was through project work, visual displays, celebrating festivals and through the medium of assemblies. Headteachers also mentioned how they shared experiences — 'If there is a major festival, for example, Ramadan, teachers do their own research, make contacts, design posters and all the pupils are involved — some are sharing their experiences while others are learning. Some of the older Muslim children tried to fast last year and the other children wanted to know what it was all about. This was, therefore, a shared experience.'

In illustrating how different cultures are expressed within the schools, a few headteachers once again stressed a distinction to be drawn between faith and culture. This distinction is evident in the following extract:

> Different cultures are expressed through assembly. We try to make sure that the material is multiethnic as opposed to multifaith. Here ours is a distinctive Christian ethos rather than a conglomeration of everyone else's as in the state schools.

Primary headteachers also provided information on whether they had made any progress in developing multicultural education in their school. Their replies are grouped under main headings in table 39.

No other question brought more varied responses from primary headteachers than the question of the progress being made in schools in the field of multicultural education. In their answers headteachers demonstrate a total lack of consensus on the aims and purposes of multicultural education. Their replies illustrate different perspectives. For some, multicultural education is concerned with 'the problem' and consequently the problem-centred approach which underlies much thinking has a direct bearing on the policies that are adopted in the school. In some schools, multicultural education is seen as synonymous with the assimilationist and integrationist approaches adopted in the 1950s and 1960s. Still more teachers see it in terms of a cultural pluralism response. Multicultural education is often seen as relevant to

Multicultural Education

TABLE 39: *Primary headteachers' replies to the question — what progress has been made in your school in developing multicultural education?*

Replies	Numbers	Percentage
None	16	43
New teaching material — books introduced	8	22
Stories, visual images, drama introduced	3	8
Teacher's example	2	5
Curriculum changes	4	11
Project work	6	16
Celebration of festivals	6	16
Christian approach — progress implicit	3	8
Teachers involved in seminars	7	19

Note: Twelve teachers mentioned more than one area in which multicultural education has progressed.

inner-city areas only and not relevant in 'white' or Christian schools.

To demonstrate the variety, extracts are given from our discussions with headteachers which depict the range of views expressed. The two main reasons for not making any progress in developing multicultural education also highlight two different perspectives. First, teachers discussed the relevance of multicultural education for their school in particular. Second, the concept of multicultural education was discussed in general terms. The view that multicultural education is relevant only because of the presence of ethnic minority groups is present in the following abstracts:

> No progress has been made because we live in this area and the children in their daily lives don't tend to come across a multicultural society... We did have some services here using a book which showed immigrants. Our children take assembly once a week and we have one prayer book with a lot of immigrants illustrated in it. The children don't see this as unnatural or odd.

Underlying this comment is the view that immigrant is synonymous with black. There is a lack of awareness that many black children are not immigrants. The presence of stereotyping is also suggested in the following abstract:

> No progress. Nothing. The community itself is isolated and we don't come across the other cultures as a regular part of the children's lives. When we have our Lent project, and this is raising money, we often look at missionary work. When children

143

Faith, Culture and the Dual System

do drawings they draw white skins. The idea of coloured skins doesn't seem to penetrate.

It is evident that a number of schools are out of touch with current thinking on multicultural issues:

> Not specifically. No overt change to the curriculum. All our kids are British born and we don't have any racial ghettos in the area, so we don't have the problems that a school is forced to meet in certain areas and perhaps that makes us lax.

> No progress has been made in multicultural education but we are aware of racist behaviour. If a child called another a paki we would deal with it immediately.

Furthermore, multicultural education was seen in terms of providing special language provision only.

> It hasn't been felt to be necessary for us to make special provision for children from other cultures because they have presented us with no special learning problems.

Another headteacher in confirming an absence of programmes for developing multicultural education said, 'We don't have any of this multicultural nonsense because we are a Christian culture.'

For other headteachers the whole principle of multicultural education was not even considered. One headteacher exclaimed 'Don't mention it. [multicultural education] The school doesn't need it just because it is the in-thing. I don't like this type of differentiation.'

However, this headteacher emphasized that 'racism' is stamped out. Another headteacher, in developing his own notion of multicultural education, illustrated the influence of the early educational responses to the arrival of ethnic minority groups:

> How do you define multicultural education? Making a mountain out of a molehill ... do not mean multiethnic, they mean West Indian or coloured. Polish and Hungarian pupils are just as likely to experience culture shock.

Clearly, what these abstracts have in common is the view that multicultural education is not relevant for all children in all schools. Its relevance is confined to schools with ethnic minority pupils.

Referring to the multicultural initiatives of local education authority one headteacher remarked:

Multicultural Education

> Our aim is to educate children. The ILEA are pursuing a separate education policy whereas our LEA is providing equal education for all its children. I wouldn't belittle a child's background but I can't go along with the LEA approach. If you had 99 per cent Bengali then I suppose you would need to look at what you are doing. Also we have such a vast variety of different cultures it wouldn't be practical to follow a separatist policy for all of them.

A headteacher in another school also perceived multicultural education as a separate time-tabled subject.

In 57 per cent of primary schools headteachers considered they had made some progress in developing a multicultural curriculum. In two schools where progress was very limited it was evident that headteachers lacked the required commitment. In the remaining schools teachers were committed to developing multicultural education and discussed with enthusiasm the changes that had occurred:

> Yes, we are making good progress and I am deeply involved. I have attended a course run by the multiethnic inspectorate. A lot of progress has been made via postage stamps, looking at the countries parents come from, the language they talk. We use a map of the world and we look at pictures of families from different countries and then locate them on the map. There have been a lot of changes in the curriculum. We always keep United Nations Day and Commonwealth Day.

Several teachers also mentioned that Commonwealth Day was a special day in their schools. When new books are introduced, teachers said that they were very careful to make quite sure that the books were not offensive to pupils and that they reflected the cultural diversity of society. Teachers said they had turned away from the traditional approach of learning everything from a 'white Christian perspective'. Examples were provided where if a class were studying clothes they would not be concerned to look at European dress only but those of other cultures. Likewise, with topics on food or the home, teachers were attempting to move away from the idea that Western European civilisation is the only culture to study. The emphasis in these schools was an understanding of cultural diversity. These changes have signalled a change in the content of the curriculum and as headteachers frequently mentioned, a change in staff attitudes.

The Rampton Report sought to identify examples of 'good practice'

145

in the field of multicultural education. The Report commends the following practice adopted by a headteacher in a primary school:

> In order to present children of all races with a positive self-image, pictures are displayed of people from other cultures in professional occupations. Stores, music, poetry and religious education from other cultures were used constantly. Our latest venture is to photograph the children's parents at their work, in their uniforms, at home and at worship, to provide our own 'local visual aids.' (p. 33)

This study encountered many examples of what the Rampton Report would see as 'good practice' at primary level.

There were headteachers who pointed out the importance of a Christian environment in contributing to multicultural education.

This view was expressed in the following way:

> Progress in developing multicultural education is implicit. There is respect for all people and this is fundamental to the Christian faith, as we are all made in God's image, therefore racism has no place. Any racist remarks are dealt with immediately on a personal level.

Other teachers also pointed out that it is part of the Christian attitude to show concern and to be aware of the different needs of pupils.

A viewpoint which places all members of the Christian faith as part of one homogenous culture is not without particular pitfalls. One headteacher commented as follows:

> The multiethnic inspectorate forget that the West Indian pupils are largely Christians even if not C of E. Their culture is often more Christian than anything else. The multiethnic inspectorate are often not aware of this (or forget about it) because they are not Christian themselves. This is not necessarily a criticism of their lack of Christianity but just an observation on the problem that ought to be realized.

Despite the evidence of progress, headteachers questioned how successful they were. In one school the deputy head went on a one-year exchange visit to the West Indians. While this visit gave the teacher a better understanding of the cultural background of the West Indian children most pupils had never been to the West Indies. This teacher worked on a project, and the school makes use of Jamaican songs, tapes and stories. The headteacher was not sure whether the exchange

Multicultural Education

helped. She commented that the West Indian teacher who came to Britain as part of the exchange also 'had problems with West Indian children who had a chip on their shoulders because they were black'. The point was also made that black children do not choose books with black faces in — as one headteacher commented, 'Putting it bluntly, these children do not gravitate to these books'.

There is a limited amount of evidence to suggest that headteachers in church schools have responded positively to multicultural initiatives that have been formulated on a diocesan level. In some schools, teachers have attended meetings and they have been involved in discussion groups which were established to look at the priorities and issues involved in developing multicultural education. However, it is difficult to discern to what extent school governors had taken policy decisions to develop multicultural education before looking for advice and help at a diocesan level.

The view that we treat all our children the same was expressed with greater frequency by teachers in church schools. 'We look for what binds us' or 'I don't believe in highlighting differences' are characteristic of the variety of forms which the justification of this sentiment takes. However, for the Swann Report and others it is 'colour blind' and 'as potentially just as negative as a straightforward rejection of people with a different skin colour and both types of attitudes seek to deny the validity of a persons identity' (p. 27). As an approach it is criticized for conveying a general unwillingness to provide accommodation for any recognition of religious, cultural and racial differences. It suggests that within a church school context, what is sauce for the Christian goose is sauce for the non-Christian gander.

It is, nevertheless, possible to discern the outlines of an alternative interpretation which takes for its starting point an equality of value in the eyes of God of all people. The Dean of Liverpool quoted in the Swann Report remarks 'The God who made the rainbow and who made the whole kaleidoscope of creation culminating in men and women of such rich variety — it is not he who is colour blind but we who find life easier to cope with if we treat it as monochrome (p. 27).' A principle which acknowledges the uniqueness and value of each child will have no place for the inclusion of a harmful self-image of any child, West Indian or other. But it must be said that there is a yawning gap between principle and practice. The principle has no room for regarding children of different faiths and cultures as being inherently superior or inferior; in practice within some schools, and in certain specific areas, the expression and recognition of pupil diversity is notable by its absence. It should be said that any multi-faith initiative or movement towards

Faith, Culture and the Dual System

dialogue, inside or outside the school, presupposes the existence of a certain level of trust. However, trust may not be assumed or called upon to order, it must be valued and it must be earned by all of the various parties involved.

'We treat them all the same' also obliquely underlines the posture adopted by educationalists both in theory and practice in matters affecting belief systems. In transferring religious belief and its everyday expression to the margin of useful activity, in pursuance of the utilitarian goal of not giving preference to any one faith, principle and practice combine to provide for balance to the rich, wholesome and diverse multicultural diet so carefully and thoughtfully prepared for pupils a uniform and ultimately unsatisfying brew of belief.

The transformation from a relatively homogenous to an essentially diverse society is reflected in the pupil composition of many church schools. Apart from the guidance and support which are available from some Diocesan Boards of Education it is notable that for church schools there are no national initiatives or agreed programmes for action in implementing multicultural education. In drawing up, or in helping to develop multicultural education, the church will manifest its care, concern and compassionate exercise of responsibility for educating the nation's children. Those individual church schools unwilling to carry out nationally agreed guidelines would accordingly isolate themselves voluntarily from the mainstream.

Our research shows that while church secondary schools lag behind county schools in the multicultural area, church primary schools have been even slower to respond.

The evidence presented in this chapter is one of institutional inactivity in 28 per cent of county schools, 34 per cent of church secondary schools and in 43 per cent of church primary schools.

It is quite clear that both church and county schools are at variance with the ideal of multicultural education set out in the Swann Report. The Report advocates that a broadly multicultural approach to the curriculum should be implemented in all schools regardless of the pupils' backgrounds.

The concept of multicultural education being of relevance to all children, including those attending 'all white' or 'all Christian' schools has failed to impinge in practice for the majority of schools in our study.

Notes

1. DES Circular 7/65.
2. The Rampton Committee was established to review the educational needs and attainments of children from ethnic minority groups. Special attention was given to the academic attainments of pupils of West Indian origin.
   See also Sally Tomlinson who provides an overview of research studies concerning ability and academic achievement of ethnic minority pupils since 1966, TOMLINSON, S. (1981) 'The educational performance of ethnic minority children' in JAMES, A and JEFFCOATE R. (Eds) *The School in a Multi-cultural Society*, London, Harper and Row Ltd, pp. 119–43.
3. *Race, Sex and Class*, 2, Multi-Ethnic Education in Schools. Inner London Education Authority, p. 23.
4. DEPARTMENT OF EDUCATION AND SCIENCE (1977) *Education in Schools: A Consultative Document*, Cmnd 6869, London, HMSO.
5. REPORT OF PROCEEDINGS (C10) (1977) Volume 8, No. 2.
6. GENERAL SYNOD OF THE CHURCH OF ENGLAND BOARD OF EDUCATION (1984) *Schools and Multi-Cultural Education. A Discussion Paper*, memorandum 2/84.
7. PHILIPS-BELL, M. (1981) 'Multicultural education: What is it?', *Multi-Racial Education*, Journal of the National Association for Multi-Racial Education (NAME) 10, 1, autumn, p. 21.
8. *Ibid*. p. 22.
9. DHONDY, F. (1982) *The Black Explosion in Schools*, Race Today Publications. Three other major critiques of multicultural education are written by: CARBY, H. (1980) in *Multicultural Screen Education*, spring; MULLARD, C. *Racism in Society and Schools: History, Policy and Practice*, Centre for Multicultural Education, University of London Institute of Education; STONE, M. (1981) *The Education of the Black Child in Britain*, London, Fontana.
10. *West Indian Children in Our Schools*, Interim Report of the Committee of Inquiry into the Education of Children from Ethnic Minority Groups, Cmnd. 8273, p. 12.
11. 1. *Rampton Committee Report*.
    2. *The Scarman Report*.
    3. *Report of the Home Affairs Select Committee*.
    4. LITTLE, W. and WILEY, R. (1981) *Multi-Ethnic Education: The Way Forward*. Schools Council Pamphlet 18.
12. *West Indian Children in Our Schools*, p. 12.
13. LEECH, K. (1984) *Insecure Foundations*, Unpublished paper, General Synod Board for Social Responsibility.

For further reading see MODGIL, S., VERMA, G., MALLICK, K. and MODGIL C. (1986) *Multicultural Education: The Interminable Debate*, Lewes, Falmer Press.

Conclusion

Those features of the dual system embodied in law which enable state and churches to offer distinctive forms of education permit both to adopt their own approaches to religious and cultural diversity in British society today.

Entering the world of education from opposite points of the compass both county and church schools have developed policies which although different in intent have some important aspects of practice in common. This is especially so in their responses to the presence of a variety of belief systems. For the most part church schools do not admit 'other faith' expression within the area of school activity and in addition they tend towards a policy of selectivity in their admission of other than Christian pupils and staff. Culture often seen as Christian, for many schools, means belonging to the historic British or European tradition. Their practice then provides what they see as the fundamental faith needs of the Christian child but leaves a void where the children of other faiths are concerned.

Some county schools have made 'tremendous' progress in their efforts to cater for the cultural diversity of pupils. Care is taken to eradicate racism and an emphasis on equality provides a mainspring for action. However, county schools have in the main responded to the 'problem' which diverse belief systems present by transferring 'belief' to the margins of useful activity.

In general, the religious or faith dimension has become a private matter for all pupils in county schools and a private matter for pupils belonging to non-Christian faiths in church schools.

It is not possible to do justice to faith without recognizing its cultural manifestations. Neither is it adequate to teach about cultural traditions without giving full recognition to their religious foundations.

The response of church schools to diversity presents a complex picture. The Church of England's contribution as a partner in education has acquired a resonant ambiguity as can be seen when the question posed in the National Society's Green Paper — to whom does the Church of England school extend Christ's welcome? — is answered in terms of the policies and practices currently adopted by church schools. For seventeen (45 per cent) church secondary and four (11 per cent) primary schools a welcome is extended to Christians only. In three of these schools it is extended to Anglicans only. Other church schools give priority to the children of the neighbourhood. This is particularly the case for many primary schools while others respond to the mechanisms of supply and demand with a series of compromises which ensure a tentative breathing space.

The historic twin aims of church schools are called into question when popular over-subscribed schools restrict pupil intake to Christian children only. The message is Christian education for Christian children. In this sense they become denominational because service to the nation is no longer a priority — the priority is to the worshipping community.

Every policy, every practice which excludes sections of the pupil population informs such groups that church schools do not 'belong' for them. As one of the main partners in the dual system the Church of England must be concerned with what is seen as its 'visible expression' in the field of educational provision in the maintained sector.

Much valuable work is published on religious education, multicultural education and other areas of interest in this study. By bringing these separate concerns together within one work it is hoped to highlight an interrelatedness which is otherwise obscured for example, the implications of staffing policy for religious education in primary schools.

The approach throughout the study is descriptive. It sets out to convey, in a general way, the overall responses encountered of church and county schools to religious and cultural diversity — and in so doing, it provides a contemporary context to help educationalists, specialists and all those concerned for the children of the nation.

Appendices

Appendix 1

TABLE 1: Distribution of Church of England voluntary-aided schools in ILEA by division and London Borough with selected characteristics of the population[1]

ILEA DIVISION	LONDON BOROUGHS COVERED	Church of England Voluntary-Aided Secondary Schools No.	Name	Percentage of the usually resident population (Census 1981)[2] In households with head born in New Commonweath or Pakistan	Born outside United Kingdom	Birthplace percentages (NHDS)[3] United Kingdom	Not in the United Kingdom	Ethnic Group Percentages (NHDS)[3] White	West Indian	African	Indian/ Pakistani/ Bangladeshi	Other	Classification of LEAs by Educational Needs (Cluster Analysis)[4] Cluster Group Code[5]	Percentage of children born outside the UK or belonging to non-white ethnic groups (indicator 1)[6]
Div. 1	Hammersmith and Fulham		Burlington Danes Lady Margaret	14.8	26.8	74.2	25.8	82.6	7.7	1.1	2.0	6.8		
	Kensington and Chelsea	3	St. Mark's	8.9	37.7	66.0	34.0	85.0	2.4	1.7	1.3	9.5		
Div. 2	City of Westminster	4	Greycoat Hospital St. Augustine's St. Marylebone Westminster City	11.5	35.7	68.0	32.0	82.6	4.3	0.7	1.6	10.9		
Div. 3	Camden		None	10.1	30.0	72.4	27.6	88.0	1.8	0.9	2.1	7.5		
Div. 4	Islington	1	Hackney Free and Parochial	16.5	24.8	76.5	23.5							
	Hackney			27.5	26.0	74.7	25.3	71.5	13.4	2.7	3.4	9.1		
Div. 5	City of London	2		3.8	18.9	80.5	19.5	89.2	0.4	0.3	–	10.0		
	Tower Hamlets		Raine's Foundation Sir John Cass and Redcoat	19.8	18.9	83.3	16.7	81.1	4.4	1.5	7.7	5.3		
Div. 6	Greenwich	1	Blackheath Bluecoat	7.9	9.5	91.4	8.6	92.7	1.8	0.4	3.3	1.8		
Div. 7	Lewisham	1	Northbrook	15.0	14.1	86.8	13.2	85.1	8.5	1.3	0.8	4.2		
Div. 8	Southwark	3	Archbishop Michael Ramsey Bacon's St. Saviour's St. Olaves	16.2	16.6	85.5	14.5	84.4	8.3	1.4	1.5	4.3		
Div. 9	Lambeth	3	Archbishop Tenison's Charles Edward Brooke St. Martin in the Fields	23.0	24.3	78.0	22.0	76.2	12.0	3.4	2.4	6.0		
Div. 10	Wandsworth		None	18.4	21.5	81.3	18.7	81.5	7.0	1.5	4.2	5.9		
ILEA (all divisions)		18											E	29

Appendices

TABLE 2: Distribution of Church of England voluntary-aided schools in the outer London Boroughs with selected characteristics of the population[1]

Outer London Borough (LEA)	Church of England Voluntary-Aided Secondary Schools No.	Name	Percentage of the usually resident population (Census 1981)[2] — In households with head born in New Commonwealth or Pakistan	Percentage of the usually resident population (Census 1981)[2] — Born outside United Kingdom	Birthplace percentages (NHDS)[3] — United Kingdom	Birthplace percentages (NHDS)[3] — Not in the United Kingdom	Ethnic Group Percentages (NHDS)[3] — White	West Indian	African	Indian/ Pakistani/ Bangladeshi	Other	Classification of LEA's by Educational Needs (Cluster Analysis)[4] — Cluster Group Code[5]	Percentage of children born outside the U.K. or belonging to non-white ethnic groups (indicator 1)[6]
BARNET	2	Christ Church C of E St. Mary's C of E	12.6	22.4	79.4	20.6	85.8	0.8	0.7	4.9	7.8	D	21
BROMLEY	1	St. Olave's	3.6	6.9	93.7	6.3	96.6	0.8	0.1	0.4	2.1	A	8
CROYDON	1	Archbishop Tenison's	11.9	13.6	87.5	12.5	88.9	2.8	0.6	3.3	4.3	D	18
EALING	1	Twyford High School	25.0	28.2	13.3	26.7	75.5	3.9	0.8	15.2	4.6	F	39
ENFIELD	1	Bishop Stopford	13.9	14.3	87.7	12.3	91.0	2.3	0.6	1.9	4.3	D	16
HARINGEY	1	School of St. David and St. Katharine	29.4	29.5	73.5	26.5	74.3	10.8	1.3	3.6	10.0	F	42
HAVERING	1	St. Edwards	2.4	4.2	96.6	3.4	98.2	0.3	0.1	0.5	0.8	A	4
HILLINGDON	1	Bishop Ramsey	6.5	9.9	91.2	8.8	93.9	0.7	0.1	3.1	1.9	D	11
HOUNSLOW	1	The Green School for Girls	16.9	19.2	82.5	17.5	84.4	1.0	0.5	9.4	4.5	D	23
SUTTON	1	Wilson's School	3.8	7.3	93.1	6.9	96.6	0.3	0.1	2.1	2.1	A	6

(Number of Church of England voluntary-aided schools in the other outer London boroughs not listed)

155

Faith, Culture and the Dual System

TABLE 3: *Distribution of Church of England voluntary-aided secondary schools outside greater London by Region/Local Education Authority, with selected characteristics of the Population[1]*

Area	Church of England Voluntary-Aided Secondary Schools No.	Name	Percentage of the usually resident population (Census 1981)[2] — In households with head born in New Commonwealth or Pakistan	Born outside United Kingdom	Birthplace percentages (NHDS)[3] United Kingdom	Not in the United Kingdom	Ethnic Group Percentages (NHDS)[3] White	West Indian	African	Indian/ Pakistani/ Bangladeshi	Other	Classification of LEA's by Educational Needs (Cluster Analysis)[4] Cluster Group Code[5]	Percentage of children born outside the U.K. or belonging to non-white ethnic groups (indicator 1)[6]
NORTH Cleveland (NMC) District: Stockton-on-Tees	1	Ian Ramsey C.E.	1.5 1.4	2.4 2.3	97.9 —	2.1 —	98.6 —	— —	— —	0.9 —	0.4 —	B —	3 —
YORKSHIRE/ HUMBERSIDE Rotherham (MD)	1	Brampton Ellis School	1.4	2.1	98.0	2.0	98.7	—	—	1.0	0.3	B	3
Calderdale (MD) Leeds (MD)	1 1	Holy Trinity C.E. Agnes Stewart C.E.	3.4 4.0	5.2 5.2	95.4 94.4	4.6 5.6	97.4 95.1	0.1 1.0	— 0.2	1.9 2.5	0.6 1.1	B B	5 8
North Yorkshire (NMC) Districts: Harrogate York	1 1	St. Aiden's C.E. Manor C.E. Sec. Mod.	0.7 0.9 1.0	3.0 4.3 3.2	97.2 — —	2.8 — —	99.4 — —	— — —	— — —	0.1 — —	0.4 — —	A — —	3 — —
NORTH WEST Bolton (MD)	1	Canon Slade School	6.4	6.2	93.7	6.3	93.3	0.2	0.4	4.7	1.5	B	10
Bury (MD) Oldham (MD)	1 2	Bury Church High Blue Coat School Crompton House C.E.	2.1 5.1	4.8 5.8	95.9 94.7	4.1 5.3	97.9 94.2	0.3 0.6	— 0.1	0.9 3.7	0.8 1.4	A B	5 10
Wigan (MD)	2	Hesketh Fletcher C.E. Deanery C.E.	0.5	1.6	98.5	1.5	99.3	—	—	0.1	0.5	B	2
Liverpool (MD)	3	St. Hilda's C.E. St. Margaret's L'pool Blue Coat	1.7	3.3	97.7	2.3	97.7	0.3	0.2	0.1	1.6	C	3

Appendices

Lancashire (NMC) Districts:	5		3.4	4.3	96.4	3.6	96.9	0.1	–	2.7	0.4	B	7
Blackburn	1	St. Wilfred's C.E.	11.4	9.2	–	–	–	–	–	–	–	–	–
Chorley	1	St. Michael's C.E.	0.9	2.4	–	–	–	–	–	–	–	–	–
Preston	1	William Temple	8.8	8.0	–	–	–	–	–	–	–	–	–
South Ribble	1	Hutton Grammar	0.9	2.6	–	–	–	–	–	–	–	–	–
Lancaster	1	Ripley St. Thomas	1.0	3.1	–	–	–	–	–	–	–	–	–
EAST MIDLANDS													
Lincolnshire (NMC) Districts:	2		0.8	3.1	97.6	2.4	99.5	–	–	0.1	0.4	A	3
Lincoln	1	Lincoln Christ's Hospital School	1.2	4.5	–	–	–	–	–	–	–	–	–
North Kesteven	1	Exeter C.E.	0.9	4.0	95.1	4.9	97.3	0.9	0.1	0.9	0.7	A	6
Northampton-shire (NMC) District:	1		2.9	5.8									
Kettering	1	Bishop Stopford C.E.	2.1	4.7	–	–	–	–	–	–	–	–	–
Nottingham-shire (NMC) District:	3		3.0	4.2	96.3	3.7	97.1	1.1	–	0.9	0.9	B	6
Ashfield	1	Hucknal National Comp.	0.4	1.4	–	–	–	–	–	–	–	–	–
Nottingham	1	Bluecoat C.E.	7.9	8.0	92.9	7.1	92.4	3.4	0.2	2.4	1.6	–	–
Newark	1	The Minister Sch.	0.7	2.6	–	–	–	–	–	–	–	–	–
			10.9	9.8									
WEST MIDLANDS (NMC)													
Birmingham (MD)	2	St. Albans C.E. St. George's C.E.	15.0	14.0	88.1	11.9	86.6	4.8	0.2	6.4	2.0	E	23
Dudley (MD)	1	Blue Coat	3.4	3.1	97.4	2.6	96.3	0.7	–	1.6	1.3	A	6
Walsall (MD)	1	Blue Coat Comp.	7.1	5.2	95.3	4.7	93.9	1.0	0.1	4.2	0.8	B	11
Wolverhampton (MD)	1	St. Peter's Collegiate	15.4	10.7	90.0	10.0	84.6	5.0	0.1	8.8	1.5	E	26
Hereford & Worcester (NMC) Districts:	2		1.2	3.3	97.2	2.8	98.6	0.2	–	0.4	0.8	A	3
Hereford	1	The Bishop of Hereford's Blue Coat	0.7	3.0	–	–	–	–	–	–	–	–	–
Worcester	1	Bishop Perowne C.E.	1.8	4.4	–	–	–	–	–	–	–	–	–

157

Faith, Culture and the Dual System

Table 3 Cont'd

Area	Church of England Voluntary-Aided Secondary Schools No.	Name	Percentage of the usually resident population (Census 1981)[2] In households with head born in New Commonwealth or Pakistan	Born outside United Kingdom	Birthplace percentages (NHDS)[3] United Kingdom	Not in the United Kingdom	Ethnic Group Percentages (NHDS)[3] White	West Indian	African	Indian/ Pakistani/ Bangladeshi	Other	Classification of LEA's by Educational Needs (Cluster Analysis)[4] Cluster Group Code[5]	Percentage of children born outside the U.K. or belonging to non-white ethnic groups (indicator 1)[6]
Staffordshire (NMC) District:	1		1.4	2.6	97.9	2.1	98.7	0.3	–	0.5	0.4	A	2
Stoke-on-Trent	1	St. Peter's C.E.	2.0	2.7	–	–	–	–	–	–	–	–	–
EAST ANGLIA													
Cambridgeshire (NMC) District:	1		2.5	6.7	93.8	6.2	97.3	0.3	–	1.1	1.3	A	7
Peterborough	1	King's School	5.8	8.5	–	–	–	–	–	–	–	–	–
Norfolk (NMC) District:	1		0.8	3.2	97.6	2.4	99.2	0.1	0.1	0.1	0.6	A	3
South Norfolk	1	Archbishop Sancroft	0.7	2.5	–	–	–	–	–	–	–	–	–
OTHER SOUTH EAST													
Berkshire (NMC) Districts:	2		6.1	9.1	92.0	8.0	94.8	1.3	0.1	2.5	1.3	A	9
Bracknell	1	Ranelagh School	2.0	6.2	–	–	–	–	–	–	–	–	–
Windsor	1	The Princess Margaret Royal Free	3.6	9.0	–	–	–	–	–	–	–	–	–
East Sussex (NMC) District:	1		1.8	5.9	95.1	4.9	98.6	0.1	0.1	0.2	1.1	A	4
Eastbourne	1	Bishop Bell C.E.	1.7	6.4	94.3	5.7	99.4	–	0.1	–	0.5	–	–
Hampshire (NMC)	1		2.2	5.3	95.4	4.6	98.5	0.1	–	0.4	1.0	A	4

158

Appendices

District/School												
District: Portsmouth	1	St. Luke's C.E.	2.4	4.9	95.1	4.9	97.4	0.1	0.1	0.5	1.8	–	–
Hertfordshire (NMC)	4		3.1	6.7	94.3	5.7	97.3	0.6	0.1	1.0	1.1	A	6
Districts: St. Albans	2	Townsend C.E.	3.4	8.0	–	–	–	–	–	–	–	–	–
Watford	1	St. Georges Parmiters Sch.	6.8	10.8	–	–	–	–	–	–	–	–	–
Welwyn	1		2.3	5.9	–	–	–	–	–	–	–	–	–
Kent (NMC)	2	Owen's School	2.3	4.7	95.7	4.3	98.4	0.1	0.1	0.7	0.7	A	5
Districts: Canterbury	1	The Archbishop C.E.	1.4	4.7	–	–	–	–	–	–	–	–	–
Tunbridge Wells	1	Bennett Memorial Diocesan Girls	1.7	5.3	–	–	–	–	–	–	–	–	–
Oxfordshire (NMC)	1		2.5	7.9	92.7	7.3	96.5	0.4	0.1	0.9	2.0	A	9
District: Oxford	1	Cowley St. John	6.7	13.0	–	–	–	–	–	–	–	–	–
Surrey (NMC)	2		2.5	7.7	92.8	7.2	98.3	0.1	–	0.5	1.0	A	5
Districts: Guildford	1	Bishop Reindorp	2.0	7.1	–	–	–	–	–	–	–	–	–
Spelthorne	1	Bishop Wand C.E.	2.8	6.3	–	–	–	–	–	–	–	–	–
West Sussex (NMC)	3		2.0	5.4	95.7	4.3	98.9	0.1	0.1	0.3	0.5	A	4
Districts: Chichester	1	Bishop Luffa C.E.	1.4	5.9	–	–	–	–	–	–	–	–	–
Crawley	1	Holy Trinity	5.3	8.0	–	–	–	–	–	–	–	–	–
Worthing	1	St. Andrew's C.E.	1.8	5.4	–	–	–	–	–	–	–	–	–
SOUTH WEST													
Avon (NMC)	2		2.4	4.2	96.2	3.8	96.9	1.0	0.1	0.5	1.5	A	5
Districts: Bristol	1	St. Mary Radcliffe and Temple C.E.	4.0	5.6	94.6	5.4	95.8	1.8	0.3	1.0	1.1	–	–
Bath	1	St. Mark's	2.5	5.8	–	3.0	99.5	–	–	–	0.4	A	3
Devon (NMC)	3		1.0	3.4	97.0									
Districts: Exeter	1	The Bishop Blackall	1.3	3.8	–	–	–	–	–	–	–	–	–
Plymouth	2	Charles C.E. St. Peter's C.E.	1.3	3.8	96.7	3.3	99.1	–	0.1	0.1	0.7	–	–

159

Faith, Culture and the Dual System

Notes

1. *Sources:* DES Computer print-out of table 1D/00 1981.
   The Education Authorities Directory and Annual, 1982
   Education Yearbook, 1982
   Individual local education authorities
   Association of Voluntary-Aided Schools
   Census 1981: selected data summarized in the Office of Population Censuses and Surveys (OPCS) County Monitors, a series of 57 pamphlets published by the Government Statistical Service.
   National Dwelling and Housing Survey: Phase 1 (HMSO, 1979) Phases II and III (HMSO, 1980).
   'A Classification of Local Educational Authorities by Additional Educational Needs (Cluster Analysis)', Department of Education and Science, Statistical Bulletin 8/82, July 1982.
2. Statistics derived from the appropriate OPCS County Monitors, table D, *Selected Characteristics of the Population*.
3. Statistics derived from the National Dwelling and Housing Survey (HMSO 1979 and 1980), Phases I, II and III, tables headed *Birthplace* and *Ethnic Group*.
4. Information derived from 'A Classification of Local Educational Authorities by Additional Educational Needs (Cluster Analysis)', DES Statistical Bulletin 8/82, July 1982.
5. Using a technique known as cluster analysis and adopting a particular similarity coefficient, on the basis of six socioeconomic indicators all local education authorities were grouped into six relatively homogenous groups (A–F), which can be summarily described as follows:
   Group A: All percentages in the 'percentage profile' below average.
   Group B: All percentages close to the average.
   Group C: All percentages in the 'percentage profile' above average except for indicator 1.
   Group D: All percentages close to the average except above average for indicator 1.
   Group E: All percentages above average.
   Group F: All percentages above average, that for indicator 1 substantially so.
   For a list of the socioeconomic indicators used see note 6 below.
6. The six socioeconomic indicators used in the cluster analysis were:
   1. Children born outside the United Kingdom or belonging to non-white ethnic groups.
   2. Children living in households whose head is a semi-skilled or unskilled manual worker or farm worker.
   3. Children living in households lacking exclusive use of one or more of the standard amenities or living in a household at a density of occupation greater that 1.5 persons per room.

Appendices

4. Children in one parent families.
5. Children in families with four or more children.
6. Pupils receiving free school meals in maintained schools.

The first five of the six indicators were derived from National Dwelling and Housing Survey data (HMSO, 1979 and 1980) by reference to the estimated number of children aged 0–17 in each authority who were covered by each factor. The information for the sixth indicator was obtained from the survey of school meals provision carried out by the DES in October 1979.

Appendix 2

TABLE 1: Ethnic composition of pupils in a sample of church and county schools

London	African	Afro-Asian	Arab	Bangladesh	Caribbean	English Scot, Welsh, Irish	Far Eastern	Greek	Indian	Pakistan	Turk	Mixture	Other
County 1	3.97	1.98	0.15	1.98	14.3	61.1	0.92	0.00	2.44	0.92	0.92	7.77	3.50
Church 1	2.63	0.00	0.00	0.00	21.9	64.1	0.00	2.65	1.43	0.00	0.20	5.69	1.43
Church (P) 1	0.00	3.96	11.2	0.00	17.7	52.6	0.00	0.65	3.96	0.00	0.00	0.00	9.88
County 2	1.81	0.00	3.44	3.26	3.98	61.6	5.43	0.36	3.81	0.72	1.27	3.60	10.7
Church 2	8.74	0.74	1.75	1.50	39.7	35.4	0.00	0.49	0.49	0.25	0.00	9.98	0.99
Church (P) 2	2.79	0.00	9.88	0.00	44.4	18.3	0.00	4.94	4.94	9.88	0.00	4.18	0.70
County 3	1.31	0.00	2.08	2.96	15.4	57.6	1.20	1.53	0.32	1.09	1.97	6.88	7.65
Church 3	6.75	0.00	1.43	2.66	7.74	68.2	2.24	1.63	3.06	1.23	0.00	2.02	3.06
Church (P) 3	2.36	0.39	3.14	0.00	1.94	68.7	2.75	0.00	0.39	3.92	0.39	3.88	12.2
County 4	6.37	1.01	2.67	5.35	14.4	54.2	2.18	0.33	2.51	0.17	4.00	4.67	2.18
Church 4	1.72	1.15	0.00	0.00	49.1	36.0	1.34	3.06	1.15	0.19	0.00	5.95	0.38
Church (P) 4	8.27	0.00	0.48	0.00	20.4	55.4	0.48	0.96	4.38	0.96	4.38	3.37	0.96
County 5	0.91	0.00	0.00	7.13	3.23	82.0	0.78	0.13	0.91	0.00	1.04	2.97	0.91
Church 5	1.46	0.18	0.00	4.39	6.01	77.3	0.00	2.56	0.36	2.38	1.64	1.46	2.20
Church (P) 5	0.92	0.00	0.00	0.00	10.1	64.9	2.76	0.00	12.1	0.00	1.84	7.43	0.00
County 6	1.62	1.08	0.00	53.6	5.59	30.1	2.53	2.17	1.08	0.00	1.26	0.53	0.36
Church 6	0.63	0.00	0.00	39.7	4.47	50.8	0.23	0.00	1.79	0.13	0.00	2.16	0.13
Church (P) 6	0.00	0.00	0.00	87.9	0.00	0.00	0.00	0.00	7.48	0.00	0.00	4.59	0.00
County 7	0.85	0.00	0.11	0.64	11.6	77.8	0.21	0.85	2.14	0.00	2.45	2.77	0.53
Church 7	3.92	0.12	0.00	0.00	28.3	60.0	0.12	3.21	1.55	0.00	0.12	1.54	1.07
Church (P) 7	11.0	4.56	0.00	0.00	46.2	31.1	0.00	0.00	0.00	0.64	0.00	5.20	1.29
County 8	2.08	0.00	0.00	1.56	8.32	74.8	2.34	1.03	2.34	0.26	4.93	2.08	0.26
Church 8	0.00	0.00	0.00	0.14	4.15	91.3	0.00	1.11	0.14	0.14	1.67	1.10	0.27
Church (P) 8	0.64	0.00	0.00	0.00	1.27	91.1	4.50	0.64	0.00	0.00	0.64	1.27	0.00
County 9	2.83	0.00	0.53	2.12	13.6	70.3	1.77	0.18	2.48	1.24	2.64	1.77	0.53
Church 9	6.46	0.25	0.00	1.55	20.4	56.9	0.00	6.46	0.25	1.81	0.51	1.53	3.87
Church (P) 9	3.33	2.86	0.47	0.00	4.26	77.7	0.00	0.47	3.33	3.33	3.33	0.94	0.00
County 10	2.70	0.00	0.00	0.00	29.7	46.3	2.70	1.73	4.05	7.50	0.95	3.25	1.16
Church 10	4.89	0.69	0.00	0.00	35.5	43.2	0.69	2.10	0.00	4.54	0.00	5.55	2.79
Church (P) 10	7.82	0.00	0.00	0.00	36.5	39.5	1.79	0.00	1.19	0.00	1.19	9.60	2.38

Appendices

TABLE 2: *Ethnic composition of pupils' backgrounds*

	African	Afro-Asian	Arab	Bangladesh	Caribbean	English Scot, Welsh, Irish	Far Eastern	Greek	Indian	Pakistan	Turk	Misture	Other
Church (S) 11	0.00	1.21	0.34	1.04	21.2	56.4	1.21	1.20	3.63	0.34	0.00	6.39	7.07
Church (P) 11	0.00	3.96	11.2	0.00	17.7	52.6	0.00	0.65	3.96	0.00	0.00	0.00	9.88
Church (S) 12	2.76	0.00	0.00	0.00	15.6	66.0	0.45	3.67	2.76	0.00	0.00	4.13	4.58
Church (P) 12	0.00	0.00	8.90	7.80	10.0	53.3	6.70	1.10	0.00	1.10	0.00	2.20	8.90
Church (S) 13	1.13	0.00	0.00	0.16	9.62	74.7	2.29	1.97	1.31	0.32	0.00	7.51	0.98
Church (P) 13	0.86	0.86	5.24	0.00	16.6	59.9	0.00	0.00	0.86	0.86	0.00	13.1	1.72
Church (S) 14	3.38	1.97	1.69	1.95	3.94	63.2	1.11	0.28	8.16	0.56	0.00	5.86	7.85
Church (P) 14	4.02	0.00	0.00	0.00	0.66	61.9	4.02	4.68	0.66	0.00	0.00	16.7	7.35
Church (S) 15	0.00	0.00	0.00	0.00	12.0	79.3	1.93	0.00	2.22	0.00	0.44	3.55	0.56
Church (P) 15	0.88	0.00	0.00	0.00	1.76	74.3	0.00	1.76	0.00	0.00	0.00	0.88	20.43
Church (S) 16	0.00	0.00	0.00	0.00	19.6	70.9	0.59	0.00	2.08	0.00	0.00	2.67	3.8
Church (P) 16	0.00	0.00	0.00	5.87	6.84	77.6	0.00	0.00	1.93	0.00	0.97	6.84	0.00
Church (S) 17	5.27	0.00	0.00	0.00	27.2	48.6	1.95	0.27	0.27	3.34	0.00	6.12	6.9
Church (P) 17	0.00	0.00	0.00	0.00	61.4	32.6	1.01	0.00	1.01	0.00	0.00	3.04	1.0
Church (S) 18	3.42	0.00	0.00	1.02	35.9	51.8	1.36	0.68	0.00	0.68	0.00	4.10	1.0
Church (P) 18	11.0	4.56	0.00	0.00	46.2	31.1	0.00	0.00	0.00	0.64	0.00	5.20	1.2

Faith, Culture and the Dual System

TABLE 3: Ethnic composition of pupils

Other London Boroughs	White	West Indian	African	Indian/Bangladeshi Pakistani	Other
County 19	97.06	.73	0.00	1.47	.73
Church 19	98.28	1.18	0.00	.39	.19
Church (P) 19	98.92	0.00	0.00	0.00	1.08
County 20	82.8	0.00	0.4	3.4	13.4
Church 20	100.0	0.00	0.00	0.00	0.00
Church (P) 20	100.0	0.00	0.00	0.00	0.00
West Midlands (2)					
County 21	21.7		13.9	64.4	—
Church 21	93.35		5.25	1.4	—
Church (P) 21	16.7		7.0	76.3	
North West Region					
County 22	3.50	—	5.45	87.16	3.89
Church 22	50.00	11.11	5.56	27.78	5.56
Church (P) 22	—	—	1.43	95.71	2.86
County 23	—	—	33.33	66.67	—
Church 23	—	44.44	—	44.44	11.11
Church (P) 23		—		100.00	—
County 24	12.20	17.07	2.44	63.67	
Church 24	8.57	13.06	11.43	63.41	
Church (P) 24	—	—	—	100.00	—

Interview Schedules and Questionnaires

Interview Schedule for Headteachers in Voluntary-Aided Secondary Schools

Background Information

History

1 Trust Deeds – Was the school specifically founded to transmit the Christian Faith and values in accordance with the principles of the Church of England?

    Yes   No   Don't Know

2 Previous status of school: Grammar
   Secondary modern
   Other

3 Present status of school: Comprehensive voluntary-aided
   Grammar voluntary-aided
   Other

4 Pupil roll

5 Is school over-subscribed?   Yes   No
Comments:

6 If Yes, how long?

7 Is school under-subscribed?   Yes   No
Comments:

8 If yes, how long?

9 What percentage of pupils make school their first choice?
What percentage of pupils make school their second choice?

10 Number of teachers

11 Religious affiliation of teachers: Church of England
   Roman Catholic
   Non-conformist
   Other
   No affiliation

Comments:

Interview Schedules and Questionnaires

12 Constitutionally, are you able to appoint teachers of faiths other than Christianity?

                                   Yes   No

Comment (for example, do they currently employ teachers of other faiths)

13 Do you have a full quota of children in:
(ILEA only)
Band 1 Yes No Band 2 Yes No Band 3 Yes No
Comment:

14 What criteria is used for admitting pupils?

15 (a) Over-subscribed situations
    (b) Under-subscribed situations

16 Are pupils interviewed before being offered a place?

                                    Yes   No

Reasons: (for example, benefit of child, school, etc.)

17 When did school last review its admissions policy?
Why?

18 Some critics of church schools have suggested that the motivation of parents to sent their children to church schools is often social and academic rather than religious — as a headteacher have you any way of knowing if this is the case?

                                   Yes   No

Reasons:

School in its Context

Area Served by School

19 Number of parishes/catchment area
Does the pupil intake reflect neighbourhood composition?
Details: Yes   No
                            Majority outside

20 What percentage of pupils use English as their mother tongue? (expand re: racial, religious, cultural, etc.)

21 What contact/relationship does your school have with the local county schools?
Headteacher:
Teachers:
Pupils:
Any ideas on developing closer ties?

22 Are pupils/teachers involved in any local community projects?
Pupils: Yes   No   Teachers: Yes   No
Details:

Faith, Culture and the Dual System

23 Is your school experiencing the effects of:
    (a) falling rolls   Yes   No
    (b) educational cuts   Yes   No
    Comments:

Aims and Objectives

School prospectus starting point for discussion
24 Priorities:
25 What is the role of your church school? How does it differ from county schools?
26 What would you say are the major Christian influences in your school?
27 Do you aim to provide children with a Christian world view?
                                     Yes   No
    Details:
28 What do you think are the short-term and long-term effects of attending a church school?
    Short-term
    Long-term
29 It is often said that teachers in church schools are searching for an expression of the Christian ideal in daily practice within the school. Can you as a headteacher identify this ideal and say in what ways your church school can give expression to it in a realistic and practical way?
    Details:

General Discussion of School Ethos

30 It is often said that the ethos of a school is not only determined by the staff but also by pupils. In your school how do:
    pupils contribute to ethos:
    teachers contribute to ethos:
31 What do you think of the National Society's suggestion of allocating non-foundation places (no Anglican connection) and foundation places (Anglican connections)?
    In principle agree
    In principle disagree
    In practice possible
    In practice impossible
    Views/difficulties (dilution of ethos?)

Interview Schedules and Questionnaires

32 Do you think that church schools have a distinctive role in our society today?
(Distinctive features of a 'good' Church of England school etc.)
                               Yes   No
Comments:
33 Do you think church schools should be an 'active Christian community linked to the church of which they are part'?
                               Yes   No
34 Is your school distinctively:
    (a) denominational in character   Yes   No
    (b) Christian in character   Yes   No
    (c) other — please specify   Yes   No

Assemblies

35 What are the aims of assembly in the school community?
Are assemblies basically:
(a) devotional
(b) linked with RE
(c) non-religious
(d) practice varies
(e) other (give details)
Content of assembly? (for example, explicitly/implicitly Christian, other?)
Discussion of difficulties:

36 How often do assemblies occur on average for each pupil?
Detailed breakdown   _____ Times per _____
                             Whole School   Year   Form/House
                                                                  (but record act
                                                                  of worship in
                                                                  classroom below)
(a) daily
(b) more than once a week
(c) once a week
(d) less frequently
Comment:

37 When there is no morning assembly do teachers normally start the day with an act of worship in the classroom?
                               Yes   No   Other
What form does it usually take: (a) Lord's Prayer
                                          (b) Hymn or psalms
                                          (c) Bible reading
                                          (d) Other (detailed)
Details:

38 What do children of other faiths do during this period/also assemblies?
39 Is Christian worship and sacramental life central in the daily/weekly experiences of the school?
                               Yes   No

Faith, Culture and the Dual System

40 Is there a school chapel?   Yes   No
41 How often does the school meet for Christian worship?

	Holy Communion/ school	School worship/ local incumbent	Church service
(a) daily	....	....	....
(b) weekly	....	....	....
(c) monthly	....	....	....
(d) once a term	....	....	....
(e) special days	....	....	....
(f) once a year	....	....	....
(g) never	....	....	....
(h) other	....	....	....

Comment:

42 Do you think Christian worship is inappropriate if the common commitment it assumes does not exist?
                               Yes   No
43 How many parents of children of other faiths/religions ask for their children to be withdrawn from assembly?
                               None   Other
Details:

Religious Education

44 As a result of RE what do you hope to achieve for pupils by the time they leave school?
45 Apart from the moral content of religious education and the general responsibility of school and teachers for the development of pupils' character is any part of the school syllabus set aside specifically for raising and dealing with moral and social questions?
Details:

Multicultural Education

46 What in your view are the aims and purposes of multicultural education?
47 What progress has been made in your school in developing multicultural education?
48 What changes have been made in the curriculum in the last three years? For example, do you incorporate an awareness of any sensitivity to racial bias, stereotyping, discrimination, racial myths etc., and an understanding of the damage they can cause?
Racism   Yes   No
Ethnocentrism   Yes   No
Comment:

Interview Schedules and Questionnaires

49 Are any teachers responsible for multicultural education?
                                Yes   No
    If yes, have they received:
    (a) in-service training
    (b) involved in working parties
    (c) attended conferences, seminars
    Numbers of teachers involved?
50 It is argued that 'some church schools emphasize their Christian basis and thereby exclude, in practice, children of other faiths thus becoming unrepresentative of their neighbourhood' (CARAF). What are your views?
51 The Runnymede Trust has suggested that church schools could 'accept some Sikh and Muslim pupils even if there were Christians wanting to attend and were unable to do so, on the grounds that to admit Asian pupils was a more important service to the local community in a racist society than to admit white ones'. What are your views?
52 Do you think that Muslims, Hindus and Sikhs should be assisted in establishing their own voluntary-aided primary and secondary schools?
                                Yes   No
    Comment:
53 What kind of pressures in society should church schools be influenced by and which should they resist?
54 Do you think that church schools should be more accountable to the dioceses?
                                Yes   No
    Comments:
55 Do you think the Church of England should give some more guidance to headteachers?
                                Yes   No
56 Do you think the Church of England should have a centrally agreed policy for all church schools?
                                Yes   No
57 As a headteacher, how closely do you work with your governing body?
58 Do you think that voluntary-aided schools should be treated in the same way as county schools in the following way:

(a) same criteria on the curriculum except RE	Yes	No
(b) same procedures for pupil admissions	Yes	No
(c) same procedures for school sizes	Yes	No
(d) staffing policy	Yes	No
(e) no power to appoint majority governors	Yes	No
(f) responsibility for non-foundation places (no Anglican connection) should be given to LEAs.	Yes	No

    Comments:
59 Sex: Male   Female
60 Age: 20–29
                  30–39

　　　　　　　40–49
　　　　　　　50–59
　　　　　　　60 and above
61　Length of time in present school as headteacher? (previous posts?)
62　Local education authority?
　　Inner London Education Authority Division:
　　Outer London borough
　　Metropolitan district
　　Non-metropolitan county
63　Diocese

General Comments

Interview Schedule for Headteachers of County Secondary Schools

Background Information

1. Previous status of school: Grammar
   Secondary modern
   Other
2. Present status of school: Comprehensive
   Grammar
   Other
3. Pupil roll
4. Is school over-subscribed?   Yes   No
   Comments
5. If yes, how long?
6. Is school under-subscribed?   Yes   No
   Comments
7. If yes, how long?
8. What percentage of pupils make school their: First choice
   Second choice
9. Number of teachers
10. Do you have a full quota of children in: (a) Band 1   Yes   No
    (b) Band 2   Yes   No
    (c) Band 3   Yes   No
    Comments

Admissions

11. What procedure is adopted?
12. Are pupils interviewed before being offered a place?
    Yes   No
    Reasons:

Faith, Culture and the Dual System

13. Has there been any change in admissions procedures in recent years?
                                   Yes   No
    Reasons:

Any likely change in admissions procedure in:
14 Over-subscribed situations
15 Under-subscribed situations

School in its Context

16 Catchment area
   Does the pupil intake reflect neighbourhood composition?
                                  Yes   No   Majority outside
   Details
17 What percentage of pupils use English as their mother tongue? (expand re: racial, religious, cultural, etc.,).
18 What contact/relationship do you have with the local voluntary-aided secondary school?
   Headteacher
   Teachers
   Pupils
19 Do you consider the relationship satisfactory?
                                  Yes   No
20 Where applicable, any views on
   developing closer ties?   Yes   No
21 Are pupils/teachers involved in any local community projects?
   Pupils: Yes   No
   Teachers: Yes   No
   Details
22 Is your school experiencing the effects of:
   (a) falling rolls   Yes   No
   (b) education cuts   Yes   No
   Details
23 Do you think that voluntary-aided schools should be treated in the same way as county schools on the following issues:
   (a) same criteria on the curriculum   Yes   No   DK
   (b) same procedure for admissions   Yes   No   DK
   (c) same procedure for school size   Yes   No   DK
   (d) same staffing policy   Yes   No   DK
   (e) no power to appoint majority of governors Yes   No   DK

Interview Schedules and Questionnaires

Aims and Objectives

School prospectus starting point for discussion
24 Priorities:
25 What is the role of your school?
    (any different from a voluntary-aided school?)
26 What in your view makes a 'good' county school?

General Discussion of School Ethos

27 It is often said that the ethos of a school is not only determined by staff but also by pupils.
    In your school how do:
    (a) teachers contribute to ethos
    (b) pupils contribute to ethos
28 In situations where a large number of pupils have made their present school their second choice do you think this has an effect on teacher/pupil morale?
    (a) teacher   Yes   No
    (b) pupil   Yes   No
    Comment:

Assemblies

29 What are the aims of assembly in the school community?
Nature of Assemblies
30 Are assemblies basically:
    (a) devotional
    (b) linked with RE
    (c) non-religious
    (d) practice varies
    (e) other (give details)
31 Content of assembly
32 Do you think that assemblies in your school should be an introduction to Christian worship?
                         Yes   No
    Comment
33 How often do assemblies occur on average for each pupil?
    Detailed breakdown   _____ times per _____
                          Whole School   Year   Form/House
    (a) daily   ....
    (b) more than once a week ....
    (c) once a week   ....
    (d) less frequently   ....

175

Faith, Culture and the Dual System

34 How many parents ask for their children to be excused from assembly? Details
35 As a result of RE what do you hope to achieve for pupils by the time they leave school?
36 What provision is made for pupils excused from RE?
37 What are your views concerning the campaign for the removal of RE and worship from state schools?
38 Would you accept that county schools can no longer be seen as agents of Christian nurture?
         Yes No DK
39 It is argued by some that children in state schools are taught all subjects from a secular viewpoint — this results in a secular approach to life and learning as the norm.
What are your views?
40 Some minority groups complain that their cultures are not taken seriously in state schools and that the devaluation of minority cultures is ingrained in the British educational system.
What are your views?

Moral Education

41 Is any part of the school timetable aimed specifically at moral education?
        Yes No
Reasons:

Multicultural Education

42 What in your view are the aims and purposes of multicultural education?
43 What progress has been made in your school in developing multicultural education?
44 What changes have been made in the curriculum in the last three years? For example, do you incorporate an awareness of and sensitivity to racial bias, stereotyping, discrimination, racial myths etc., and an understanding of the damage they can cause?
racism   Yes No
ethnocentrism   Yes No
Comments:
45 Are any teachers responsible for multicultural education?
        Yes No
If yes, have they received: (a) in-service training
         (b) involved in working parties
         (c) attended conferences, seminars
Number of teachers involved?

Interview Schedules and Questionnaires

46 Sex   Male   Female
47 Age   20–29   30–39   40–49
               50–59   60 and over
48 Length of time in present school as headteacher? (previous posts?)
49 Local education authority?
     ILEA Division
     Outer London borough
     Metropolitan district
     Non-metropolitan county
50 Diocese.

General Comments

Interview Schedule for Religious Education Teachers in County and Voluntary-Aided Secondary Schools

Provision

1. How many periods per week are timetabled for religious education at each stage of the school?

	Forms 1–2	Forms 3–4	Forms 5–6
Number of periods per week			
One period per week	....	....	....
Two periods per week	....	....	....
More than two periods per week	....	....	....

2. Do you use a prescribed syllabus for RE?

                                    Yes   No

   If yes, which syllabus (or syllabuses) is followed?

3. What is the status of RE in the school curriculum?

Aims and Objectives

4. As a result of RE what do you hope to achieve for your pupils by the time they leave school?
5. As a result of RE do you hope that pupils will have a clear understanding of Christian morality?
6. As a result of RE do you hope that pupils will be more sympathetic to other religions?

                                    Yes   No

   Comments

7. Is RE in your school concerned, in particular, with developing a religious outlook?

                                    Yes   No

   Comments

Interview Schedules and Questionnaires

8   Do you think that an aim of RE is to nurture the personal faith of its young adherents?

                                                   Yes   No

    Comments

9   Do you agree that the aims of the RE syllabus in a church school are the same as those of a county school but will be developed within the context of a Christian community?

                                                   Yes   No

    Comments

10 What should be the aim of RE in a society whose religious outlook is pluralist?

11 Do you agree that it is not the task of the county school to initiate children into a religious faith?

                                                 Yes   No

    Comments

12 Do you think that RE should have the effect of positively encouraging children to become Christians?

                                               Yes   No

    Comments

13 If a pupil asked — is Christianity the one true religion? What would you say?

Content

14 In your school does Christianity remain the cornerstone of religious teaching?

                                               Yes   No

    Comment

Voluntary-Aided Schools Only

15 Is RE in your school centred on:
    (a) the teaching of the parent church
        (church teaching)   Yes   No
    (b) is it 'core Christianity' common to the main
        denominations (basic Christianity)   Yes   No
    Comments

16 Are pupils prepared for confirmation?

                                               Yes   No

    Comments

17 Are religions other than Christianity dealt with in RE classes?

	Forms 1–2	Forms 3–4	Forms 5–6
Yes, specific provision	....	....	....

Faith, Culture and the Dual System

    Yes, as the occasion arises   ....
    No, or rarely   ....
    Cannot say   ....

18 If so, does the choice of religions studied reflect the faiths of pupils?

                                                                 Yes   No

    Details

19 What religious education is provided for children of other faiths?

20 Do you include 'other stances for living' in RE classes?

    Which ones:

Humanism	Yes	No
Marxism	Yes	No
Others	Yes	No

    (please specify)

    Reasons

21 Are any pupils withdrawn from RE?

    If yes, what provision is made for pupils excused from RE classes?

                                                                  Yes   No

    Provision — details

    Reasons for withdrawal

Approach to RE

22 What approach to RE is adopted in your school?

23 In your school is religion taught as something to be investigated rather than embraced?

                                                Yes   No

    Comments

24 Is it possible for RE in your school to do justice to the different religious backgrounds of pupils?

                                                Yes   No

    Comments

25 Do you think that children of different faiths should be taught by teachers professing the same faiths?

                                                Yes   No

    Comments

26 Do you think that it is possible for a teacher/pupil who does not hold a particular faith to enter into the experience of it?

Teacher	Yes	No
Pupil	Yes	No

    Comments

Interview Schedules and Questionnaires

General

27 Should RE in church schools differ from county schools in:
    (a) aims   Yes   No   DK
    (b) approach   Yes   No   DK
    (c) content   Yes   No   DK
    Comments

28 RE that is concerned with Christian nurturing and teaching for commitment within the community of faith is justified because the child is better able to understand other religions. (pupil-centred)
    What are your views?   Agree   Disagree
    Comments

29 'The presence of adherents of other faiths has acted as a catalyst and created the question of social justice in the teaching of religion'.

30 Do you let pupils know that you are committed to certain beliefs?
                                Yes   No
    Comments

31 Number of pupils taking examinations in RE:
                          CSE
                        'O' level
                        'A' level
    Comments

32 Do you think that a subject that is not examined lacks status?
                                Yes   No
    Comments

33 Number of qualified teachers?

34 Age group   20–29
                       30–39
                       40–49
                       50–59
                       60+

35 Length of time in present post

36 Sex   Male
               Female

37 Area: ILEA Division
        Outer London borough
        Metropolitan district
        Non-metropolitan county

Faith, Culture and the Dual System

Church Schools Questionnaire

Part 1

1	Sex	Male
		Female
2	Age	20–29
		30–39
		40–49
		50–59
		60+
3	Present post	Headteacher
		Deputy headteacher
		Scale 2 or above
		Scale 1
4	School	Primary
		Secondary
5	Type of school	County
		C of E aided
		C of E controlled
		C of E special agreement
		C of E independent
		Inter-denominational
6	Prior to taking up your present post, have you taught on a permanent basis in these types of schools	County
		C of E aided
		C of E controlled
7	*County school teachers only*	
	In the area where you teach is there a C of E voluntary-aided secondary school	Yes No

Interview Schedules and Questionnaires

8   Religious Affiliation

	Committed	Nominal

   Church of England
   Roman Catholic
   Other Christian denominations
   Hinduism
   Sikhism
   Islam
   Other
   (Please specify)

Part 2

Please indicate whether you agree or disagree with the following statements.
If you *strongly agree* circle   SA
If you *agree* circle   A
If you are *not certain* circle   NC
If you *disagree* circle   D
If you *strongly disagree* circle   SD

9   The C of E should hand over its schools to the state, with the exception of church involvement in religious education   SA A NC D SD
10 The C of E must be involved in education   SA A NC D SD
11 One dimension of the church's mission is 'the betterment of human life'   SA A NC D SD
12 Education is so permeated with values that the church has its own unique and distinctive contribution to make   SA A NC D SD
13 It is a worthwhile pursuit of the C of E to maintain separate church schools   SA A NC D SD
14 The church and the school can no longer be partners in Christian nurture   SA A NC D SD
15 Church schools should be more accountable to:
    (a) Local education authorities   SA A NC D SD
    (b) Diocesan directors   SA A NC D SD
16 Church schools should be treated in the same way as county schools on the following issues:
    (a) same criteria on curriculum except for RE   SA A NC D SD
    (b) same criteria on *whole* curriculum   SA A NC D SD
    (c) same procedure for admissions   SA A NC D SD
    (d) same procedure for school size   SA A NC D SD
    (e) same staffing policy   SA A NC D SD

Faith, Culture and the Dual System

17	The C of E's withdrawal from the dual system is undesirable	SA	A	NC	D	SD
18	As long as parents want church schools they should exist	SA	A	NC	D	SD
19	Parents have a priori right to choose the kind of education that shall be given to their children	SA	A	NC	D	SD
20	Church schools in single school areas should be transferred to LEA control	SA	A	NC	D	SD
21	Church schools are a poor return on investment of time and money	SA	A	NC	D	SD
22	The C of E as the established church should have concern for all schools not special influence in some	SA	A	NC	D	SD
23	There is something special about a church school which is valuable and significant	SA	A	NC	D	SD
24	Teachers in church schools are searching for an expression of the Christian ideal in daily practice within the school	SA	A	NC	D	SD
25	Church schools should be more accountable to the C of E	SA	A	NC	D	SD
26	The C of E should have a generally agreed policy for all church schools	SA	A	NC	D	SD
27	One of the aims of a church school is 'to enable pupils to understand Christianity and see the Christian faith applied'	SA	A	NC	D	SD
28	The church school 'provides the opportunity of parental choice for Christian nurturing	SA	A	NC	D	SD
29	Interviewing prospective pupils is 'a hidden form of selection' and cannot be justified	SA	A	NC	D	SD
30	Interviewing prospective pupils works in the interest of the pupil	SA	A	NC	D	SD
31	The disadvantages of interviewing prospective pupils far outweigh the advantages. Therefore it should be discontinued	SA	A	NC	D	SD
32	Church schools have outlived their usefulness	SA	A	NC	D	SD
33	Church schools should give priority to children with special needs	SA	A	NC	D	SD
34	Church schools should give priority to children of practising Anglicans	SA	A	NC	D	SD
35	Church schools should give priority to parents who want a Christian education for their children	SA	A	NC	D	SD
36	Church schools are racially divisive	SA	A	NC	D	SD
37	Church schools are socially divisive	SA	A	NC	D	SD

Interview Schedules and Questionnaires

38	Church schools should encourage pupils to accept and practise the Christian faith	SA	A	NC	D	SD
39	Church schools have a distinctive contribution to make to education and nurture of children	SA	A	NC	D	SD
40	There is a distinctive Christian view of education that can properly be expressed in a church school	SA	A	NC	D	SD
41	The C of E should invest in more secondary schools because there is an imbalance between primary and secondary provision	SA	A	NC	D	SD
42	Teachers in Church schools are shielded from the harsh realities of unemployment	SA	A	NC	D	SD
43	Religious education in Church schools should differ from that of a county school	SA	A	NC	D	SD
44	'Committed Christians in county schools are doing a different job from RE teachers in church schools'	SA	A	NC	D	SD
45	County schools are no longer seen as agents of Christian nurture	SA	A	NC	D	SD
46	Church schools are inward-looking communities shut off from the secular world	SA	A	NC	D	SD
47	Church schools must, as a first priority, be concerned with the identity of Christian faith and life	SA	A	NC	D	SD
48	Schools must underline the rightful place of Christianity at the centre of any RE syllabus devised for use in this country	SA	A	NC	D	SD
49	Church schools perpetuate social discord to an extent that makes them indefensible	SA	A	NC	D	SD

Interview Schedule for Headteachers in Primary Voluntary-Aided Schools

Background Information

History

1 Trust Deeds — was the school specifically founded to transmit the Christian faith and values in 'accordance with the principles of the Church of England'?

                            YES   NO   UNCERTAIN

Size

2 Pupil roll
3 Is the school over-subscribed?   YES   NO   N/A
4 If yes, how long?
5 Is the school under-subscribed?   YES   NO   N/A
6 If yes, how long?
7 Number of teachers
8 Religious affiliation of teachers
9 Constitutionally, are you able to appoint teachers of faiths other than Christianity?

                            YES   NO

    Comments:

Admissions Policy

10 What criteria is used for admitting pupils?
     Reasons:
11 Are pupils interviewed before being offered a place?
                             YES   NO
     Reasons:

Interview Schedules and Questionnaires

12 What would happen in the event that the school was:
(a) over-subscribed (b) under-subscribed
Comments:
13 Do you think that admissions policies for church voluntary-aided primary schools should give priority to the children in the neighbourhood, whatever their denominational allegiance/children from other faiths etc.
YES   NO
Reasons:

School in its Context

Area Served by School

14 Number of parishes/catchment area:
Does the pupil intake reflect neighbourhood composition?
YES   NO   MAJORITY OUTSIDE
Details:
15 What percentage of pupils use English as their mother tongue? (expand re: racial, religious cultural etc.)
16 Aims and objectives of school
17 What is the role of your church school?
18 Is your school concerned with laying the foundations for an understanding and possible acceptance of a particular religious tradition?
YES   NO
Comments:
19 As a result of RE what do you hope to achieve for pupils by the time they leave school?
20 Is there a distinctive element of religious education in the work of the infant school or not?
YES   NO
Comments: (syllabus used?)
21 What are the aims and purposes of religious education in your school?
22 Content of religious education
23 What religious education is provided for children of faiths other than Christianity?
24 How are different cultures and faiths expressed within your school?
25 What progress, if any, has been made in your school in developing multicultural education?
PROGRESS   YES   NO
26 Do most children attend your school with the hope of going to secondary Church of England school?
YES   NO
Comments:
27 Aims, and content of worship

Faith, Culture and the Dual System

28 Discussion of practical difficulties
29 What do children of non-Christian faiths do during school worship?
30 Does your school operate as an extension of the parish church?
    YES   NO
    Comments:
31 Is the local incumbent Chairman of the Governors?
    YES   NO
32 What partnership exists between headteachers/pupils and local incumbent?
    (a) regular visits to school
    (b) regular church services
    (c) other
    Details:

Headteacher

33 Sex   Male   Female
34 Age   20–29   30–39   40–49
               50–59   60+
35 Length of time in present school as headteacher
36 Local education authority?
        Inner London Education Authority Division
        Outer London borough
        Metropolitan district
        Non-metropolitan county
37 Diocese
    See list of dioceses

Questionnaire for Local Education Authorities

Information required from Local Education Authorities
Please circle yes or no as appropriate. Add comments only if you think it is necessary. **We guarantee strict confidentiality**

1 **Catchment Area**
   County Schools Only
   (a) Do you have a catchment area policy?   Yes   No
   (b) If yes, is the policy that pupils should attend the   Yes   No
   geographically nearest school?
   (c) Please specify if the policy is other than geographically nearest school
   Comment:

2 **Multicultural Provision**
   (a) Has your Authority formulated any policies concerning   Yes   No
   multicultural education?
   If yes, would you be kind enough to send us any literature you have on these policies.
   (b) Do you have a multicultural inspector/adviser?   Yes   No
   (c) Do you have a multicultural resource centre?   Yes   No
   (d) Do you employ section 11 teachers?   Yes   No
   If yes, how many? .....
   (e) Do you employ teachers of English as a second language? (please state if these posts have section 11 support):
      (i) in schools   Yes   No
      (ii) in separate language centres   Yes   No
   Comment:
   (f) Do you employ staff to develop communication skills in   Yes   No
   mother tongue?
   (g) Do you make other multicultural provision?
   If yes, please specify:

3 **Composition of Population**
   As our project is particularly concerned with church schools in a multi-

cultural, multiracial and multifaith society, we would like to collect statistics on the ethnic composition of pupils. **We stress that any information provided will remain absolutely confidential.**

(a) Do you collect information on ethnic minority children in your authority using the Home Office definition of 'Commonwealth immigrant' (Home Office Circular No. 97/1982, re: section 11 of the local government Act 1966) or any other definition?
Yes   No

(b) If yes, would you be willing to provide us with statistics both on the ethnic composition of the total pupil population in your Authority and in the individual schools included in our project?
Yes   No

(c) If yes, ideally we would like to gather the information under the categories used by the National Dwelling and Housing Survey and would ask you, if possible, to complete the table below. If you are unable to do this, could you provide the information we require in any other form and attach it to this questionnaire? We have included a similar question on our separate divisional questionnaires asking for this information for each of the individual schools included in our projects.

School	White	West Indian	African	Indian/ Bangladeshi/ Pakistani.	Other	All Pupil

4 Can we list your Authority among the sixteen local education authorities which have contributed to the project. **We guarantee strict confidentiality.** No views/information will be attributed to specific authorities or schools.
Yes   No

Thank you for your assistance.

Diocesan Directors — Questionnaire

1. Do you advise/recommend a particular admissions policy for church voluntary-aided schools in your Diocese? If so, what is the philosophy underlying this admissions policy?
2. Do you see any of your church schools as neighbourhood schools (defined as serving the local community regardless of pupil's religious background)? Do you see a difference on this issue between your primary and secondary schools?
3. What are your views on the National Society's suggestion of allocating foundation places (Anglican connections) and non-foundation places (no Anglican connections) in terms of admissions? Please relate to schools in your diocese.
4. Have you advised headteachers to adopt a foundation/non-foundation scheme?
5. Do you intend to advise headteachers to adopt such a scheme?
6. If a foundation/non-foundation scheme was introduced, do you think responsibility for non-foundation places should be given to LEAs?
7. What do you see as the role for church schools in education today? Do you preceive any difference between the role of church primary and church secondary schools?
8. Although in theory the role of the diocese in education is 'advisory', how much influence do you, as the Diocesan Director of Education have in practice, in your voluntary-aided schools?
9. Is there usually a representative of the diocese on the governing bodies of its voluntary-aided schools?
10. Do you think church schools should be more accountable to the diocese?
11. Have you formulated any new initiatives for your schools during the last three years, for example, has the diocese encouraged inter-faith dialogue? If so, could you please specify.
12. How many church schools are there in the diocese?
    Primary: voluntary-aided.....
               voluntary-controlled......
               special agreement.....

191

Secondary: voluntary-aided.....
voluntary-controlled.....
special agreement......

13 Can we list your diocese among the nine dioceses involved in the project? *We guarantee strict confidentiality.* No views/opinions will be attributed to specific dioceses.

Questionnaire for Parents

1 Did your child attend a Church of England primary school?
2 Why did you choose a Church of England secondary school?
   Reasons
   (a) Wanted a Church of England education
   (b) Good academic reputation
   (c) Good discipline
   (d) Wanted a Christian education
   (e) Nearest school
   (f) Social reasons
   (g) Medical reasons
   (h) Single-sex school
   (i) Other
3 If more than one reason ASK
   Which reason do you consider the most important?
4 As a result of RE what do you hope this school will achieve for your child by the time he leaves?
5 Do you wish your child to participate in Christian worship within the school?
                                         Yes   1   No   2
6 Did you consider a county school education for your child?
                                           Yes: voluntary   1
                                           Yes: form requirement   2
                                           No: 3
   If YES
   What factors decided you to choose a church school?
   If NO
   Reasons for not considering a county school.
7 Many parents associate church schools with 'good discipline'. Do you rate 'good discipline' as an important factor in this school?
                                         Yes   1   No   2
8 What do you see as 'good discipline'?

Faith, Culture and the Dual System

9 Did you receive a church school education?
   Mother: Yes 1   Father: Yes 1
           No 2   No 2
10 If YES, is there anything about your church school education that you have come to value?
11 Religious affiliation
   Mother
   Father
12 Country of origin
   Mother
   Father
13 Interviewee
   Mother   1
   Father   2
   Both   3
14 Parent of first year pupil   1
   Parent of prospective pupil   2
   Parent of pupil who will start in September   3

Index

A levels 91, 94
academic knowledge, religious education 96–7
academic reputation, church schools 37–8, 66
admission policies 9, 17–30
  church schools 31–5, 51–2
  effects of 1980 Education Act 34
  headteachers 45
advocacy, religious education 119, 120
African children 5
agnostics 74
Allington Statement 35–7, 50
Anglican *see* Church of England
Asian families 44
Asian pupils 41, 42, 44
Asians 98
assemblies
  aims of 74–5
  county schools 70–2
  non-religious 84
  withdrawal from 81
assimilationist approach, to multicultural education 127–8, 136, 141–2
atheist teachers 110
atheists 74

balance of ability formula 23, 64
banding 23, 33, 47, 64–5
Bangladesh 43

Bangladeshi children 5
Bangladeshis 5
baptism 22
Baptists 28
Barnet 2, 6
behaviour, development 111–12
beliefs 85
Bible 79
Birmingham 6
Birmingham Agreed Syllabus 89
Birmingham diocese 6
black Christians 41
black churches 108
black pupils 39, 143
Blackburn 6
Blackburn diocese 6
Board for Mission and Unity 51
Bolton 6
British Council of Churches 51, 120, 121
Bromley 2, 6
Buddhism 102, 106, 110, 114, 122, 123
Buddhists 28, 50, 79

Camberwell papers 102
Canterbury diocese 6
Caribbean Pentecostalism 81, 108–9
Caribbean pupils 41, 42
carol services 82
catchment areas

195

Index

church secondary schools 25
schools 17–18, 43, 127–8
census, 1981 4
Central Advisory Council for Education 110
Certificate of Secondary Education 91, 93, 97, 123
Chelmsford diocese 6
children, ethnic minority groups 5
Christian content, assemblies 71–2, 73
Christian morality 75–6, 102–5
Christian nurture 89, 97, 98–101, 118, 120, 121–2
Christian voluntary groups 99–100
Christian worship 69, 83–4
  assemblies 75–6
  church schools 76–9
Christianity 89, 106, 107, 120, 122, 123, 124, 125, 146, 151
  as true religion 116–17
  central place in religious education 101–2, 112–13
  committment to 114–15
  grounding in 95
  pluralism 108–9
  relations with other faiths 50–1
  understanding of 111–12, 113–14
Christians, admission priority 27
Christmas 111
church attendance 22
church membership, school admission 21
Church of England 9, 29, 50, 112, 129, 141
  active membership 21
  church school provision 18–20
  primary schools 1, 2
  schools 35–7
  schools policy 36–7
  teacher membership 55–6
Church of England Board of Education 129, 140
Church of England voluntary-aided primary schools 6–7, 11, 29

Church of England voluntary-aided schools, distribution 154–9
Church of England voluntary-aided secondary schools 1, 2, 3–4, 6–7, 8, 10, 11, 23, 29, 31–2, 37–8
church primary schools 55, 57
  admission policies 26–9
  ethnic composition 41–2, 43, 44–5
  links with church 82
  over-subscribed 28–9
church schools
  ability groups 64–5
  admission policies 17–30, 31–5, 51–2
  approach to religious education 115–17
  as white enclaves 40, 44, 45
  assemblies 73–5
  collective worship 76–9
  ethnic composition 40–5
  links with church 82–3
  multicultural education 131–48
  nature and purpose 48
  over-subscribed 21, 22, 23–4, 26, 47, 52, 63
  'poaching' 35
  potentially divisive nature 38–40
  pupil intake 26
  questionnaire 185–8
  relationship with county schools 32–3
  religious education 90, 91–2, 117–19
  response to diversity 151–2
  selectivity 59–67
  staff appointments 55–9
  teacher perceptions 9
church secondary schools 55, 57
  catchment areas 25
  ethnic composition 41
  links with church 82–3
  pupil rolls 31–2
church services, compulsory attendance 83
Cole, W. 105

Index

Coles, O. 98
collective worship 84
  church schools 76-9
  statutory basis 69-70
colour blind approach, to ethnic diversity 135
Commission for Racial Equallity 46
Commonwealth Day 145
communicants, Church of England 56
communism 110
community, primary school links with 27-8
community education courses 92
community of faith 83
comprehensive schools 1, 66
confirmation 22
Confucianism 106
consequential dimension, religious expression 85
Coptics 28
counties 3
country of birth classification, census data 4
county schools
  ability groups 64-5
  admission policies 17-30
  approach to religious education 115-17
  assemblies 70-2
  ethnic composition 40-5
  multicultural education 131-48
  over-subscribed 18
  pupil intake 26
  religious education 90-1, 92, 117-19
  school services 82
  social disadvantage 59-64
  under-subscribed 26
county secondary schools 1, 2, 10-11
  pupil rolls 31-2
Cracknell, K. 86
Crowther Report 110
Croydon 2, 6
CSE 91, 93, 97, 123

cultural diversity 42, 151
  approach to multicultural education 128-9, 130, 132-4, 142-3
cultural pluralism 85
culture, religion and 85-6
curriculum
  multicultural education 132, 133
  religious education in 93

Dancy, J. 78
decision-making, church schools 36
Department of Education and Science 2, 3, 4, 19, 129
  Plowden report 112
  Rampton Report 137, 139, 145-6
  Swann Report 69-70, 106, 119, 128-9, 134, 138, 139, 142, 147, 148
DES Statistical Bulletin 8/82 4, 5
Dhondy, Farrukh 130-1
Diocesan Boards of Education 129-30, 141, 148
Diocesan Directors 20
  questionnaire 195-6
Diocesan Education Committees 19-20, 36
Diocesan Education Officers 2
direct grant grammar schools 43
discipline, church schools 66
doctrines 85
Durham Report 83, 84, 96, 114
Durkheim, E. 103

Ealing 2, 6
Easter 111
Education Act (1944) 20, 29, 33, 69, 76, 83, 84, 89
Education Act (1980) 17, 33, 34
educational aims, assembly 74-5
educational cuts 32, 33
educational deprivation 5
educational needs, immigrant pupils 128-9
elucidation, religious education 119, 120

197

Index

Enfield 2, 6
English as a second language 40
entrance examinations, selective schools 18
equality, in education 129
ESL provision 40
ethnic composition, schools 40–5, 162–4
ethnic minority groups 28, 40, 131, 135, 143
ethnic origin 4–5
ethos, school 78, 103–4
examinations, influence of 97
experiental dimension, religious expression 85

faith 85
  community of 83
faiths, non-Christian 50–1, 73, 79–81, 83
fascism 40
Festival of Lights 79
foundation and non-foundation places, church schools 45–8, 49–50
free school meals, eligibility 59–61, 67

GCE 91
General Synod of the Church of England Board of Education 19, 50, 51, 129, 140
Gerloff, R. 108
Glock, C.Y. 85
good behaviour, development 111–12
governing bodies
  church schools 36, 68
  staff appointments 55–9
governors 8
  church schools 19–20, 33, 35, 120
grammar schools 1, 66
Greater London 73
Green, R. 39–40

Haringey 2, 6
Havering 2, 6

headteachers 7–8, 10
  admission interviews 24–5, 28
  admission policies 18, 20–2, 34, 45
  Allington Statement 35–7, 50
  assemblies 70–2, 74–5
  categories of assemblies 71–2
  church schools 20, 55
  church secondary schools 35–7
  county schools 32–3
  foundation and non-foundation places 46–8, 49–50
  impressions of pupils' ethnic background 40–1
  interview schedules 167–79, 189–91
  primary schools 43
  relationship with church 82–3
  religious education 111–14
  school worship 75–80
  staff appointments 55–9
  views of multicultural education 131–48
Hillingdon 2, 6
Hindu pupils 73, 80, 83, 138–9
Hindu teachers 57
Hinduism 102, 103, 106, 107, 122, 123
Hindus 27, 28, 44, 45, 47, 50, 79
Holy Communion 82, 83
Hounslow 2, 6
Humanism 109
humanities courses 92
Humanities Curriculum Project 131
hymns 72, 73

ideological dimension, religious expression 85
immigrant pupils 127–9
immigrants 143
in-service training, RE teachers 106
India 43
Indian children 5
Indians 5
indoctrination 101, 117
Inner London Education Authority 1–2, 3, 6, 23, 31, 32–3, 59, 62, 64,

Index

129, 138, 140, 154
integrationist approach, to multicultural education 128–9, 131–2, 141, 142
intellectual dimension, religious expression 85
interview schedules, headteachers 167–79, 189–91
interviewing, school admission 24–5
interviews
    primary school admission 28
    research study 7, 9
Islam 102, 103, 105, 106, 107, 108, 122, 123, 125

Jehovah's Witnesses 81, 94
Jenkins, Roy 128
Jewish teachers 57
Jews 28, 50, 79, 107
Joint Education Policy Committee 19
Joseph, Sir Keith 70
Judaism 106, 122, 123

Koran 79, 122

Lamb, C. 86
Lancashire local education authority 5
languages
    ethnic minority groups 40
    ILEA schools 42
Lichfield diocese 6
living, non-religious stances 109–10
local education authorities 9–10, 17–18, 30, 33, 35, 41, 140–1, 144–5
    questionnaire 193–4
London and Southwark Diocesan Boards of Education 2
London boroughs, outer 2–3, 155
London diocese 6, 29

McIntyre, J. 86
maintained schools 10–13
Manchester diocese 6
Maoism 109
Martin, D. 50

Marxism 109
medical reasons, for admission 34–5
Methodists 28
Metropolitan districts 3, 6
mission, school worship 78–9
morality 103, 115
    Christian 75–6
multicultural education 10, 80
    approaches 127–9
    concept 130–1
    policies 129–30
    secondary schools 131–41
multicultural society, education for 130
multifaith education 79–80
Muslim assembly 79
Muslim pupils 67, 73, 80, 81, 83, 113
Muslims 24, 27, 28, 43, 44, 45, 47, 50, 94, 105, 108, 122, 124, 136

National Dwelling and Housing Survey 4, 5
National Society 18–19, 20, 29, 46, 48–9, 50, 51, 152
NCWP origin 4
New Commonwealth or Pakistan origin 4
Newbigin, Bishop 51
Nichols, K. 79
non-foundation places, church schools 45–8, 49–50
non-manual workers, parental occupations 63–4
non-Metropolitan counties 3
non-Metropolitan districts 6
North-West region 3–7, 42, 43, 44, 73
nurture, Christian 89, 97, 98–101, 118, 120, 121–2

O levels 91, 93, 123
occupations, parental 62–4, 67
Office of Population Censuses and Surveys 4, 5
Oldham 6

199

Index

Oneness Pentecostals 109
Orthodox Jews 28
outer London boroughs 2–3, 155

Pakistan 44
Pakistani children 5
Pakistanis 5
parental occupations 62–4, 67
parental unemployment, county schools 64
parents 8
  admission interviews 24–5, 28
  aims of religious education 114–15
  attitudes to religious education 93
  choice of church school 37–8
  preference for religious foundation 21
  questionnaire 197–8
  school preferences 17–18, 34, 35
parishes, primary school catchment area 27–8
Passover 79
Pentecostalism 108–9
Pentecostalists 28, 81
Pentecostals Healing Movement 109
personal faith, lack of 99
Philips, D.Z. 119
Philips-Bell, M. 130
Plowden report 112
postal questionnaires, research study 8, 9
prayers 72, 73
Preston 6
primary school pupils, religious background 27, 28
primary schools 1, 2, 10–11, 55, 57
  Church of England 1, 2
  ethnic composition 41–2
  free school meals 60–1
  multicultural education 141–8
  over-subscribed 28–9
  religious education 111–14
problem-centred approach, to multicultural education 142
pupil admission policies 9, 17–30

pupil intake
  neighbourhood composition and 26, 27
  selective 59–67
pupil rolls, falling 31–2, 33, 35
pupil-centred aims, religious education 95–6
pupils
  admission interviews 24–5, 28
  ethnic backgrounds 162–4
  religious affiliation 73–4
  religious background 27, 28, 123
  religious diversity 79–81
  social backgrounds 59–64

questionnaires
  church schools 185–8
  diocesan directors 195–6
  local education authorities 193–4
  parents 197–8
  research study 7, 9

race 4–5
Race Relations Board 137
racial disadvantage 66
racial equality 129
racial groups 40
racism 40, 66, 67, 97, 98, 129, 132, 133, 137, 138, 146
racist behaviour 138–9, 144
Ramadan 142
Rampton Report 137, 139, 145–6
Rastafarians 28
Registrar General 62
religion
  defining ethnicity 5
  ways of expression 85
religions
  non-Christian 122–3
  world 92, 105–7
religious affiliation
  pupils 73–4
  school admission 21
  teachers 56–7
religious aims, assembly 74–5

Index

religious background, pupils 27, 28, 123
religious beliefs 85
   multiplicity 84
   pluralism 70
religious community, church school as 67
religious content, assemblies 71–2, 75
religious diversity 67, 79–81, 99
religious education 9, 70, 77, 85, 134–5
   aims and objectives 95–8
   approaches 115–17
   difference in church and county schools 117–19
   integrated 57, 92
   primary schools 111–14
   secondary schools 90–2
   status 92–4
   statutory basis 89
   withdrawal from 81, 94–5
Religious Education Departments 10
religious education teachers 7, 8, 9, 91–110, 113, 116–19, 122–5
   interview schedules 181–4
religious experience 85
religious outlook 96
religious pluralism 113
   secular response 119
religious understanding 115
rites 83, 85
ritualistic dimension, religious expression 85
Rochester diocese 6
Rodger, A.R. 109, 110
Rogers, R. 35, 38
Roman Catholic schools 45
Roman Catholics 28, 47
Runnymede Trust 39, 66–7
Rutter, M. 78

sacramental life 83
school meals, free 59–61, 67
school services 82
school worship 69–86
schools
   ethnic composition 40–5
   ethos 103–4
Schools Council 85, 101, 109, 116, 117, 119, 131
secondary schools 55, 57
   admission policies 17–26
   ethnic composition 41
   free school meals 60
   multicultural education 131–41
   over-subscribed 18
   religious education 90–2
secular effects, of religion 85
secular outlook 99
secular response, religious pluralism 119
selective schools 18
Sikh pupils 67, 73, 83
Sikh teachers 57
Sikhism 107, 123
Sikhs 27, 44, 45, 50, 80, 124
single-parent families, pupils from 61–2, 67
social aims, assembly 74–5
social backgrounds, pupils 59–64
social class 62–4
social disadvantage, county schools 59–64
social studies 92
Socialist Education Association 59, 66
society-centred aims, religious education 97–8
socio-economic indicators, disadvantage 5
South Ribble 6
Southwark Diocesan Board of Education 130
Southwark diocese 6
special agreement schools 14
special reasons, for admission 34–5
staff appointments, church schools 55–9
Stark, R. 85
Sunday Schools 124

Index

Sutton 2, 6
Swann Report 69–70, 106, 119, 128–9, 134, 138, 139, 142, 147, 148

Taoism 106
teachers 8
  appointment 55–9
  Christian 67
  non-Christian 56–7
  religious education 91–110, 113, 116–19, 122–5, 181–4
  responsibility for multicultural education 140
tolerance 97, 98, 100–1
Trinitarian Pentecostals 109
Trust Deeds, church schools 20

underachievement, West Indian pupils 128
unemployment, parental 67
United Nations Day 145

voluntary groups, Christian 99–100
voluntary-aided primary schools 6–7, 29
voluntary-aided schools 14
voluntary-aided secondary schools 1, 3–4, 6–7, 8, 10, 11, 23, 29, 31–2
voluntary-controlled schools 14

Watson, B. 96, 120
West Indian forms, Christianity 108–9
West Indian pupils 5, 81, 136, 139, 146–7
  underachievement 128
West Indians 39
West Midlands 3–7, 42, 43–4, 73, 140
Wolverhampton 6
world religions 92, 105–7
worship 76